Explore

CCSS/PARCC Prep
Grade 6 Reading

by Dr. James E. Swalm and Dr. June I. Coultas
with Patricia Braccio and Kathleen Haughey
Edited by Ralph R. Kantrowitz and Sarah M.W. Espano
Designed by Nancy C. Goroff

Queue, Inc • 80 Hathaway Drive • Stratford CT 06615
Phone 800 232 2224 • Fax 800 775 2729

www.qworkbooks.com

THE AUTHORS

Dr. James Swalm has been actively involved in the development of classroom instructional materials for many years. As Director of the New Jersey Right to Read and Bureau of Basic Skills, he participated in the development of statewide tests in reading, writing and mathematics as well as in the writing of various instructional and staff development materials in reading and language arts. Dr. Swalm has authored and co-authored numerous books and professional articles on reading, writing, and assessment, as well as on the use of technology in instruction. He has taught both undergraduate and graduate level courses in reading and curriculum development, and at all levels, K–12. Dr. Swalm has also been a principal, assistant superintendent, and superintendent, and has served as an educational consultant to many school districts.

Dr. June I. Coultas is well-known in the field of education and curriculum development. Her many positions include that of teacher, director of curriculum and instruction, college professor, consultant, lecturer, and award-winning grant writer. She is the author and co-author of numerous educational books, as well as of multimedia software programs. Her career includes being New Jersey director of the federal Right-to-Read Program, and manager of the state Bureau of Basic Skills. In addition to memberships in numerous professional associations, she is a past president of the New Jersey Reading Association.

Acknowledgments
Illustrations
Carl W. Swanson, Ph.D.
Maureen B. Coultas
Sarah J. Holden
Margaret Paulson

Student Book ISBN: 978-0-7827-2342-7 • Class Pack ISBN: 978-0-7827-2343-4 • Copyright © 2014 Queue, Inc.

Table of Contents

Tips for Answering Multiple-Choice Questions

Multiple-choice questions have a **stem,** which is a question or an incomplete sentence, followed by four answer choices. You should select only one answer choice. Here are some tips to help you correctly answer multiple-choice questions on the Common Core English Language Arts Test:

- Read each passage carefully.
- Read each question and think about the answer. You may look back to the reading selection as often as necessary.
- Answer all questions on your answer sheet. Do not mark any answers to questions in your test booklet.
- For each question, choose the best answer, and completely fill in the circle in the space provided on your answer sheet.
- If you do not know the answer to a question, skip it and go on. You may return to it later if you have time.
- If you finish the section of the test that you are working on early, you may review your answers in that section only. Don't go on to the next section.

Checklist for Answering Open-Ended Questions

- Keep the central idea or topic in mind.
- Keep your audience in mind.
- Support your ideas with details, explanations, and examples.
- State your ideas in a clear sequence.
- Include an opening and a closing.
- Use a variety of words and vary your sentence structure.
- State your opinion or conclusion clearly.
- Capitalize, spell, and use punctuation correctly.
- Write neatly.

CHAPTER 1

Text Elements
Theme, Central Idea, and Supporting Details

RSL.6.1, RSI.6.1: RECOGNITION OF CENTRAL IDEA OR THEME
RSL.6.2, RSI.6.2: RECOGNITION OF SUPPORTING DETAILS

Reading helps you to learn and to communicate. A story that you read could introduce you to people, places, and ideas that you might never have met otherwise. By reading stories and passages, you probably know how to identify **themes**, **central ideas**, and **supporting details**.

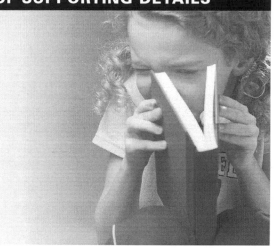

In some of the stories in this workbook, you will be able to identify a theme, or a universal truth about life. Throughout the workbook you will be asked to identify the theme, or central idea, and supporting details of different stories or passages.

YOU TRY IT

You have just finished reading a book you checked out of the school library. Your teacher asks you to do an oral book report in which you must tell the class the central idea of the story.
• Do you tell them everything that happened in the story?
• Do you identify the important characters?
• Do you write why the author wrote the story?
• Do you write what you think the story was about?

To come up with your best answer, think about what the story is trying to communicate. What is the main message in the story? See if you can explain the story's message in one sentence or less.

RSL.6.1, RSI.6.1: RECOGNITION OF CENTRAL IDEA OR THEME

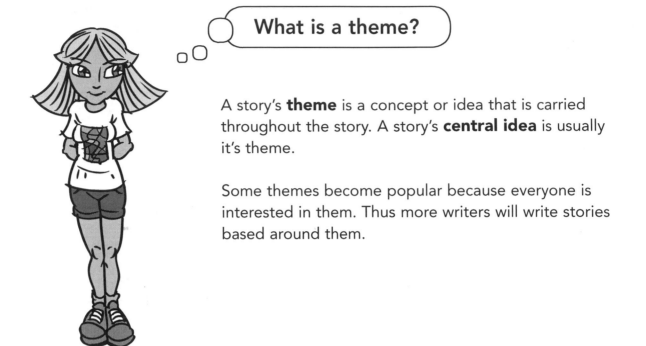

What is a theme?

A story's **theme** is a concept or idea that is carried throughout the story. A story's **central idea** is usually it's theme.

Some themes become popular because everyone is interested in them. Thus more writers will write stories based around them.

Here are some ways to find a theme:

• Look at each sentence in the passage or story and think about whether or not it is important to the story as a whole. Would the meaning of the passage or story change if this sentence was removed?
• Try to write a headline of less than five words to sum up the point of the passage.
• Imagine that you are going to tell a friend about this story. What would you tell him or her?

What are some common themes in literature?

• Human vs. Nature
• Love and Friendship
• Self-Awareness
• Rites of Passage

RSL.6.2, RSI.6.2: RECOGNITION OF SUPPORTING DETAILS

What are supporting details?

Supporting details are ideas or information that build upon or explain the central idea.

An author will use supporting details to help get his or her point across, to explain his or her point of view. These details could be facts or additional parts of the story that build upon the idea.

If you identify the central idea first, it will probably be easier for you to then determine which sentences include the supporting details.

Read the example below showing supporting details:

Abraham Lincoln best described democracy as "government of the people, by the people, and for the people." For a government to be "by the people," however, requires that the people decide who shall be their leaders. Without free and fair elections, there can be no democratic society. The right to vote, therefore, is not only an important individual liberty; it is also a foundation stone of free government.

The central idea of this paragraph is that, in order for people to live in a democracy, they must have the right to vote. The supporting details are:

• Abraham Lincoln described democracy as "government of the people, by the people, and for the people."
• In a democracy, the people must be able to choose their leaders.
• Elections must be free and fair.
• The right to vote is important for each person who lives in a democracy.
• One of the foundation stones of free government is the right to vote.

LET'S TRY IT TOGETHER

A Bundle of Sticks from Aesop's Fables

A father had a family of sons who were very often quarreling among themselves. When the father failed to heal his sons' disputes with his advice and encouraging words, he determined to give them a practical illustration of the evils of fighting all the time. For this purpose, one day he told them to bring him a bundle of sticks.

When they had done so, he placed the bundle into the hands of each of them in turn and ordered them to break it in pieces. Each one tried with all his strength, but was not able to do it.

The father next opened the bundle, took the sticks separately, one by one, and again put them into his sons' hands, upon which they broke them easily.

He then addressed them in these words: "My sons, if you are of one mind and unite to assist each other, you will be as this bundle, uninjured by all the attempts of your enemies; but if you are divided among yourselves, you will be broken as easily as these sticks." ∎

What is the central idea of this story?

Is it that the father's sons were always arguing with each other?
No, that is not the central idea. Although it is the way the fable begins, it does not tell us what the entire story is about.

Is it that the father told his sons to bring him a bundle of sticks?
The fact that the father told his sons to bring him a bundle of sticks is a supporting detail. However, it is not the central idea.

Is it that the father asked each son to break the sticks?
The fact that the father asked each son to break the bundle of sticks into pieces is another supporting detail, but not the central idea.

Is it that the sons were being injured by their constant fighting?
Yes! That is the central idea of the story. If you look at the entire story, you will notice that all of the details go back to and support this idea.

What is the theme of this story?

Is it that it's easier to break one stick than a bundle of sticks?
No. Although the father in the fable does show his sons that this is true, this is not the theme.

Is it that it often helps, when trying to get a big task done, to break it into smaller parts first?
No. Although the fable does show that it is easier to accomplish a large task if it is broken into smaller parts first, this is not the theme.

Is it that banding together creates strength?
Yes! That is the theme of the fable. The lesson the father hopes to share is that his sons could do more if they worked together. By using the bundle of sticks as an example, or metaphor, he is demonstrating that he would like his sons to understand the importance of family unity.

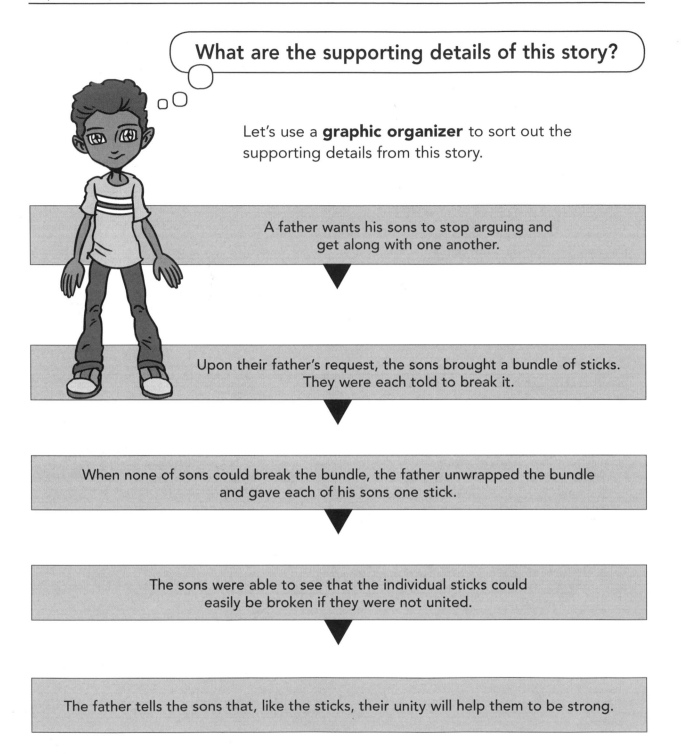

What are the supporting details of this story?

Let's use a **graphic organizer** to sort out the supporting details from this story.

A father wants his sons to stop arguing and get along with one another.

Upon their father's request, the sons brought a bundle of sticks. They were each told to break it.

When none of sons could break the bundle, the father unwrapped the bundle and gave each of his sons one stick.

The sons were able to see that the individual sticks could easily be broken if they were not united.

The father tells the sons that, like the sticks, their unity will help them to be strong.

YOU TRY IT

DIRECTIONS INTRODUCTION	Read this story/passage and answer the questions that follow. Years ago, people who were blind could only learn through listening. Then Louis Braille developed a system that allowed blind people to read.

Louis Braille

1 Louis Braille, the inventor of the Braille reading system, was born in France in 1809. Right from the beginning, people noticed that Louis was a bright, inquisitive child. These characteristics lead both to a tragic accident when Louis was four and to his ability later on to overcome the problems caused by this accident.

Simon-René Braille, Louis's father, owned a harness shop in their village, and Louis loved to play with his dad's tools. One day, he was playing in his father's shop with a sharp tool called an "awl." Somehow, the sharp end of the awl struck his eye.

At first, the doctor thought that Louis's eye would heal. However, it didn't and the wound became infected. The infection spread, causing Louis to completely lose sight in both eyes.

At first, Louis was devastated. Within a short time, though, he began to adapt and was soon leading a relatively normal life. He even went to school with his friends; he learned by listening to the teacher. Louis was so bright that he was still able to keep up with the other children.

At the age of 10, he received a scholarship to attend the French School for Blind Youth in Paris. In this new school, Louis learned most of the time by listening. The principal of the school had developed a system for blind people to use so they would be able

✔ CHECK FOR UNDERSTANDING

Why do you think the author mentions Braille's curiosity throughout the passage?

read books. It was difficult to use, though, and none of the textbooks had been written in this system. Students could still only learn by listening to the teachers.

Nonetheless, the school did have 14 books in the library that had been written so that blind people could read them. The print in the books was raised and the students could run their fingers over the letters to read. This process was laborious, it took so long to read each page that few students bothered with these books.

Louis, however, read all of these books. While mastering the raised print, he realized that a more efficient system was sorely needed. At the same time, Louis also learned to play the cello and organ, and music became his first love. Soon many Paris churches wanted him to be their organist.

When Louis was 12 years old, Captain Charles Barbier de la Serre spoke at the school about an alphabet he had developed. Barbier had invented a system to make it possible for soldiers to read and write messages at night without any light. He called his system "night writing." Barbier's code of 12 raised dots represented words by sound rather than by spelling.

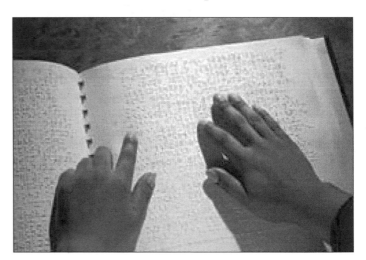

Over the next few months, an idea began to take shape in Louis's mind. He quickly saw the potential of using a code with raised dots that would allow blind people to read. However, Barbier's 12-dot code was cumbersome. Louis also felt that using the sounds of words rather than the actual spelling made reading more difficult. The dilemma he wrestled with was how to develop a code that was simple to use and that allowed a book to be read rapidly.

While Louis was home on vacation, he got the idea that allowed him to develop his own code. He was sitting at his father's workbench and began fingering the same type of tool that had caused his blindness. Louis felt the tip of the awl and realized that it was blunt. It was at that moment that an idea flashed through his mind. He would use the awl to punch holes into paper. Now all he needed was a simpler code.

 Explore CCSS/PARCC Grade 6 Reading © 2014 Queue, Inc. All rights reserved.

Louis set about making an easier code. He developed a six-dot code that could be used to represent all the letters of the alphabet and the necessary punctuation marks. As soon as he had the code, he proceeded to punch holes representing words into a piece of paper. Then he punched in groups of words. In each case, he was able to read what he had written. Finally, Louis wrote a sentence in his new code and then proceeded to read it.

Louis's writing system provided a quick way to make books readable by blind people. Very soon after he developed the letters, he developed a code that could be used to write music that could be read by blind people. The first book in braille was published in 1827 under the title *Method of Writing Words, Music, and Plain Songs by Means of Dots, for Use by the Blind and Arranged for Them.* In 1839, Louis published details of a method he had developed for communication with sighted people, using patterns of dots to approximate the shape of printed symbols.

Louis Braille became a teacher at the School for the Blind in Paris. He remained at the school for the rest of his life. However, the system he had developed so that blind people could read was not widely accepted. Not until after Braille died in 1852 was the practicality of the system recognized. Today, Louis Braille's system bears his name and is used in every country in the world. ■

1. Which of the following best describes Louis Braille?

   A. creative but lazy

   B. bright and carefree

   C. fair but frightened

   D. intelligent and determined

HINT: This question asks you to identify the theme of the passage. Think about what you have read. What do you think was the common message throughout?

2. What caused Louis Braille's blindness?

   A. He hit his head on his father's workbench.

   B. He spent too much time trying to read in the dark.

   C. He got poked in the eye with a sharp tool.

   D. He got into an accident while away at school.

HINT: This question asks you to recall a detail from the passage. If you are unsure of the answer, reread the second paragraph.

3. What is a theme of "Louis Braille"?

   A. Good friends help each other through tough times.

   B. Anything is possible if you try hard enough.

   C. It's better to tell the truth than it is to lie.

   D. It's important to fight for what you believe in.

HINT: This question asks you to identify the theme of the passage. Think about what you have read. What do you think was the common message throughout?

4. Which of the following gave Louis Braille the idea for his Braille system?

   A. a special code he used with his father

   B. a language that used hand motions to talk

   C. a system used by soldiers to read at night

   D. an alphabet used to teach blind students

HINT: This question asks you to recall a detail from the passage. If you are unsure of the answer, reread the middle of the passage.

5. Why did Louis Braille make the Braille system using a six-dot code?

   A. The six-dot code fit better when printed on paper.

   B. The twelve-dot code was in a different language.

   C. The six-dot code had fewer letters in its alphabet.

   D. The twelve-dot code was too difficult to learn.

HINT: This question asks you draw a conclusion from the passage. If you are unsure of the answer, skim the passage to look for clues.

6. The purpose of the first paragraph is to

   A. describe the childhood of Louis Braille.

   B. foreshadow events in Louis Braille's life.

   C. explain Louis Braille's tragic accident.

   D. discuss the accomplishments of Louis Braille.

HINT: This question asks you to identify why the author wrote the first paragraph. If you are unsure of the answer, reread the paragraph. What did it tell you?

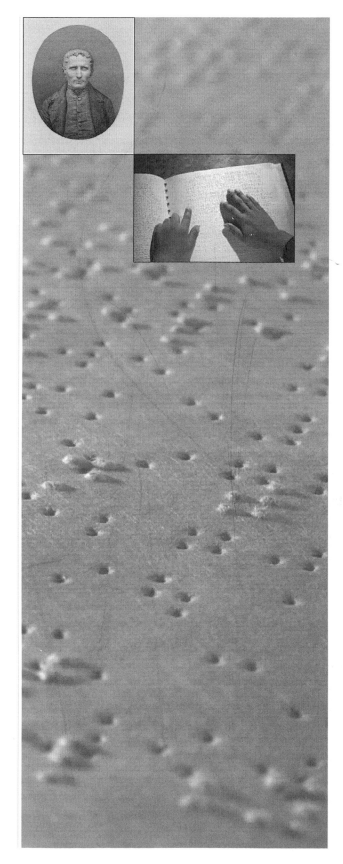

7. **Despite his injury, Braille possessed qualities that made it possible for him to overcome his disability and go on to help others all over the world.**

   • **List three of Louis Braille's personal qualities, and briefly explain how each one contributed to his accomplishments.**

   Use specific information from the article and any additional insight to support your response.

8. Great advances have been made in the fields of medicine, education, and science to benefit people since the early 19th century.
   • How are blind or visually impaired people able to function in today's society in ways that would not have been possible in Louis Braille's time? Explain.
   Use specific information from the article and any additional insight to support your response.

YOU TRY IT

DIRECTIONS INTRODUCTION	Read this story/passage and answer the questions that follow. The Paralympics is a major sporting event that parallels the Olympics. At these unique games, people that are disabled are given the opportunity to compete in events that display their physical abilities.

The Paralympics

The Paralympics is the Olympics for disabled athletes. It is the second largest sporting event in the world. Only the Olympics are larger.

How the Paralympics Started

Sir Ludwig Guttmann, a British brain surgeon, is the father of the Stoke Mandeville Games/Paralympics. In 1944, Guttmann was asked by the British government to found the National Spinal Injuries Centre in Stoke Mandeville near London, at the Stoke Mandeville Hospital.

Dr. Guttmann felt that, with training, the veterans with spinal injuries at the hospital could potentially learn to live normal lives in regular society. He used sports as a way for these people to strengthen their bodies. Soon, he noticed that the men and women also began to feel better about themselves as they played the games.

The first sports Guttmann taught the people to play were archery and table tennis. Then, the patients began asking for team sports, and interest increased once they had been started. More patients asked to be in the classes. The men and women rarely missed a class that involved team sports.

5

In 1948, the first archery competition took place among the disabled athletes. Many of the veterans watched as the archers competed against each other. They then asked Guttmann to hold competitions in all the sports that he had arranged to be played at the hospital. In a short time, similar games were set up with other hospitals in England.

✔	CHECK FOR UNDERSTANDING

How do you think the Paralympics are beneficial to the athletes and their families?

These games were very successful. Families of the disabled athletes watched with pride as the games were played. The athletes felt good about how they played in the games because they felt that they could finally lead productive lives.

Guttmann decided to organize a larger competition with more games. The games would only be for wheelchair athletes. He called these games the Stoke Mandeville Wheelchair Games. They were held at the same time as the Summer Olympics in London.

Paralympics and the Olympics

The Stoke Mandeville Games became an annual event. In 1952, athletes came from many countries to compete. The games were so successful that others were started. Soon, games for disabled athletes began to be held all over the world.

In time, the term "Paralympics" began to be used for these wheelchair games; it was used to mean "games for paraplegic athletes." (Someone who is paraplegic has lost the use of his or her legs.) After a while, however, the meaning of the word changed. People began to think of games for world-class athletes with a wide range of disabilities. The prefix Para- began to mean "parallel." People thought that these games paralleled the Olympics. Today, the word Paralympics means "parallel Olympics." Only the schedule and number of events are modified. There is both a summer and a winter Paralympics.

9

The big breakthrough came in 1960. During that year, the Paralympics were held in Rome, Italy. Over 400 paraplegic athletes from 23 countries participated. The games were run just like the Summer Olympic games. World-class athletes competed for gold, silver, and bronze medals.

Paralympics games have been held every Olympic year since 1960. Starting in 1976, the first Paralympics Winter Games were held in Sweden. Also beginning that year, blind athletes and amputees were included in the games. Today, five types of disabilities are represented in the games. These include those athletes who are blind, in wheelchairs, amputees, dwarfs, or have cerebral palsy. In 2010, the events of the Paralympics Winter Games – to be held in Vancouver and Whistler, Canada – will be: Alpine Skiing, Nordic Skiing, Wheelchair Curling, and Sledge Hockey.

In 1988, another major change occurred. Korea agreed to hold the Paralympics two weeks after the regular Olympics. The disabled athletes used the same fields and stayed in the same facilities as the Olympic athletes. At the Albertville Winter Games in 1992, the Winter Paralympics and the Winter Olympics were held at the same site for the first time. In 2000 in Sydney, Australia, almost 4,000 athletes from 125 countries competed in 18 events, the biggest Paralympics ever.

Special Olympics and Paralympics

Many people confuse the Paralympics with the Special Olympics. The two are very different. The athletes in the Special Olympics have mental and cognitive problems. Their games focus on participation. People from eight to 80 years old are welcome to take part. In the Special Olympics, everyone who enters is a winner and receives prizes. On the other hand, the Paralympics are for elite competitors. They must follow similar guidelines to their Olympic counterparts. Medals are awarded only to the winners.

Summary

Today, Olympic officials run the games. World-class disabled athletes compete following the same rules as the Olympics. In the future, additional groups of disabled athletes will probably compete in the games. ■

1. **Why did Dr. Guttmann use sports to help injured veterans?**
   A. He thought sports would help to strengthen their bodies.
   B. He thought sports would help to make them more relaxed.
   C. He thought sports would encourage them to work with others.
   D. He thought sports would show them how to overcome problems.

   HINT: This question asks you to think about information from the passage. If you are unsure of the answer, reread the beginning of the passage for clues.

2. **What caused increased interest in Dr. Guttmann's program?**
   A. people with different disabilities joining the program
   B. the fact that table tennis was added to the program
   C. the fact that team sports were added to the program
   D. the program being held during the Summer Olympics

   HINT: This question asks you to think about information from the passage. If you are unsure of the answer, skim the section "How the Paralympics Started" and look for a mention of an increase in participation.

3. **In paragraph 5, the word "competed" means**
   A. fought.
   B. talked.
   C. complimented.
   D. played.

   HINT: This question asks you to identify the meaning of the word "competed." Reread paragraph 5. Are there any clues to the word's meaning in the paragraph?

4. **How did the Stoke Mandeville Games differ from other competitions for disabled athletes?**
   A. The Stoke Mandeville Games were not held every year.
   B. The Stoke Mandeville Games were only for wheelchair athletes.
   C. The Stoke Mandeville Games did not have very many events.
   D. The Stoke Mandeville Games were only for athletes from England.

   HINT: This question asks you to draw a conclusion from the passage. You need to go beyond what is stated there and figure out how these games were unique.

5. According to the paragraph 9, the term "paraplegic" means a person has lost the use of his or her

   A. arms.

   B. hands.

   C. neck.

   D. legs.

HINT: This question asks you to identify the meaning of the word "paralympics." Reread paragraph 9. Are there any clues to the word's meaning in the paragraph?

6. What does the term "Paralympics" mean today?

   A. only for wheelchair athletes

   B. only for blind athletes

   C. parallel Olympics

   D. special Olympics

HINT: This question asks you to recall a detail from the passage. If you are unsure of the answer, reread paragraph 9.

7. What major change to the Paralympics occurred in 1976?

   A. Athletes with other disabilities entered the Paralympics.

   B. Athletes from all over the world entered the Paralympics.

   C. The Paralympics were run just like the Summer Olympics.

   D. The Paralympics were held after the Summer Olympics.

HINT: This question asks you to recall a detail from the passage. If you are unsure of the answer, skim the passage looking for a mention of the year 1976.

8. Why did the author most likely write this passage?

   A. to explain how the Paralympics differs from the Special Olympics

   B. to describe what all athletes must do to take part in the Paralympics

   C. to tell readers about the history of the Paralympics

   D. to show readers how the Paralympics are run today

HINT: This question asks you to identify the author's purpose. Think about what you have read. Why do you think the author wrote this passage?

9. Dr. Ludwig Guttmann directed the treatment of spinal injuries and "used sports as a way for these people to strengthen their bodies." The benefits of physical activity and sports go well beyond making people's bodies stronger and more fit.

• What are the other ways that people are helped by their participation in sports and physical activities? Explain.

Use specific information from the article and any additional insight to support your response.

10. In order to express the elite performance and the strong will of every Paralympian, "Spirit in Motion" became the Paralympic motto in 2003.
    • Who is eligible to participate in the Paralympics? Explain.
    • Do you think that the Paralympic motto could also apply to athletes participating in the Olympics and the Special Olympics? Explain.
    Use specific information from the article and any additional insight to support your response.

YOU TRY IT

DIRECTIONS **INTRODUCTION**	Read this story/passage and answer the questions that follow. The Great Lakes have had an extremely high number of shipping accidents and mysterious disappearances. These highly traveled waterways have long puzzled fisherman, business owners, and locals.

The Mysterious Great Lakes

The five Great Lakes are a very large freshwater transportation system in the northern part of the United States, between the United States and Canada. Many ships carry cargo to ports on the five lakes. Some also travel through the St. Lawrence Seaway to ports on the Atlantic Ocean. Yet, many of these ships have left ports and have never been seen again. Over the past 300 years, thousands of ships have been lost, some with their entire crews.

The explorer René Robert Cavelier de la Salle's ship, *Griffin*, was one of the first large ships to sail the Great Lakes. It was completed and launched in 1679 by La Salle and his carpenters to transport the furs from the animals his men had trapped in the wilderness. The *Griffin* successfully set sail up river and into Lake Erie on August 7, 1679. Carrying a crew of 32 men, the *Griffin* began its historic voyage across the uncharted waters first of Lake Erie, and then up the Detroit and St. Clair Rivers into Lakes St. Clair and Huron.

The St. Clair River was difficult for the vessel to navigate because of both the strong current and a gale blowing off Lake Huron. The crew literally walked the banks of the river, pulling the ship along with ropes. The *Griffin* entered Lake Huron on August 23rd. It was on this lake that the ship encountered a furious gale. The storm eventually eased and the *Griffin* arrived safely at a small settlement at St. Ignace. There was much celebration at the straits and the ship remained anchored there until September 12th, when La Salle set sail for La Grand Baie, the old name for Green Bay, Wisconsin. The *Griffin* set sail for Niagara on September 18th and was never seen again. La Salle remained behind. The vessel was under the command of a man named Luc and five sailors. They never arrived.

Drawing of the Griffin

The explorer René Robert Cavelier de la Salle

The number of ships lost on the Great Lakes is staggering. In 1871, 1,167 disasters were recorded. Between 1878 and 1898, 5,999 vessels were wrecked. Of this number, over a thousand were total losses. Collisions, explosions, and fires have caused many of the shipwrecks. However, many also have been caused by the lethal storms that occur suddenly on the Great Lakes.

These storms are measured by their wind speeds:

- **Gales:** declared when the wind speed reaches a speed of 39 miles per hour
- **Storm:** when the wind speed reaches 55 miles per hour; this is the highest rating given to any wind disturbance on the lakes even if the wind reaches hurricane force. The fiercest storm was gauged at 103 miles per hour.

November seems to be the worst month for storms and shipwrecks on the lakes. Since 1835, 19 of the 20 disturbances classified as storms occurred in November, the month the sailors do not like to sail on the lakes. Sometimes, these storms rage for days and take numbers of ships with them. For instance, the Great Storm of 1913 raged over four days, sank 20 ships, and damaged dozens more.

The most famous ship sunk during the month of November 1975 was the *Edmund Fitzgerald*. This ship and its crew of 29 suddenly disappeared on Lake Superior, 17 miles from Whitefish Point, Michigan. This site is the location of Whitefish Point Light Station, the oldest lighthouse on Lake Superior, and the Great Lakes Shipwreck Museum. Whitefish Point is in an area known as the "Graveyard of Ships." Hundreds of different ships lie on the bottom of the bay and nearby.

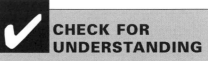

✔ **CHECK FOR UNDERSTANDING**

Why do you think the people living in the Great Lakes area are so interested in these mysterious cases?

Using sonar, the wreckage was found four days later. She was broken in half in 535 feet of water. The ship, barely 20 years old, was one of the largest of its type in use on the Great Lakes and it featured the latest technology. The reason for her sinking remains one of the great mysteries of the lakes. Canadian folk singer Gordon Lightfoot wrote a ballad in 1976 entitled *"The Wreck of the Edmund Fitzgerald."* Author Michael Schumacher compiled *Mighty Fitz: The Sinking of the Edmund Fitzgerald*, published in 2006.

Surviving a Great Lakes storm is still a challenge, even with today's technology. These storms can explode across hundreds of miles of open water with little or no warning. Often, storms on the Great Lakes cause more navigational problems than storms on the oceans. One reason is that the storms often appear very quickly, almost out of nowhere.

In some instances, ships that were caught in these storms barely had time to radio for help before sinking. A second reason is that the waves in the Great Lakes jump and strike quickly. This jumping and striking action results in more pounding of a ship during a storm. They are not the rolling, swelling types typical to ocean storms.

Edmund Fitzgerald

The five lakes also react differently to the storms. Lake Erie is the lake most captains like the least. It is the shallowest and has a muddy bottom. This causes problems with navigation in both good and bad weather. Lake Superior is the largest and deepest lake and is liked by most captains. The large size provides room for maneuvering during a storm. However, its rocky coastline and huge waves (caused by its great depth) present problems not found in the other lakes. Captains feel that Lake Michigan is the trickiest of the lakes to navigate. The prevailing winds constantly sweep across it and cause different currents. They are particularly evident in the Straits of Mackinac. These currents make it the most difficult lake for a ship to stay on course. One lake even has a special area where very unusual things occur. Lake Huron has a deadly stretch of water called the Marysburgh Vortex. This strip of water has a long history of bizarre ship losses, some of which defy explanation.

10

Some people think of these five lakes as a place similar to the Bermuda Triangle. These people point out that there have been even more strange happenings in the Great Lakes than in the waters off Bermuda. There also have been more ships lost in the Great Lakes than in the Bermuda Triangle.

Despite all of these bizarre occurrences, most of the time, ships travel these waters safely. Authorities feel that books written about these incidents have contributed to some of the mystery that surrounds the loss of some ships. Many ships have passed through these lakes during storms and, at worst, have suffered only minor damage. ∎

1. **René Robert Cavelier de la Salle built the *Griffin* to transport**
   A. people.
   B. furs.
   C. wood.
   D. rocks.

   HINT: This question asks you to recall a detail from the passage. If you are unsure of the answer, reread the second paragraph.

2. **Why do storms on the Great Lakes cause more navigational problems than storms on the ocean?**
   A. Winds are much harsher on the Great Lakes.
   B. Storms form quickly over the Great Lakes.
   C. Temperatures are much colder on the Great Lakes.
   D. Waves appear suddenly in the Great Lakes.

   HINT: This question asks you to think about information from the passage. If you are unsure of the answer, reread the information related to surviving a Great Lakes storm.

3. **The purpose of paragraph 6 is to**
   A. explain which month is most dangerous for sailors on the Great Lakes.
   B. tell about the cargo transported by many of the ships on the Great Lakes.
   C. describe what happened to the Edmund Fitzgerald on the Great Lakes.
   D. show what it is like to experience a storm while sailing on the Great Lakes.

   HINT: This question asks you to identify why the author wrote a certain paragraph. Reread paragraph 6. What was the author trying to tell you about?

4. **How are the waves on the Great Lakes different from the waves on the ocean?**
   A. The waves on the Great Lakes roll and swell.
   B. The waves on the Great Lakes are not very quick.
   C. The waves on the Great Lakes jump and strike.
   D. The waves on the Great Lakes are not very large.

   HINT: This question asks you to draw a conclusion based on the passage. What did the passage say about the waves on the Great Lakes and those on the ocean?

5. Which of the lakes is preferred by most captains?
   A. Lake Erie
   B. Lake Huron
   C. Lake Michigan
   D. Lake Superior

HINT: *This question asks you to recall a detail from the passage. If you are unsure of the answer, reread paragraph 10.*

6. What does the word "maneuvering" mean in paragraph 10 of the passage?
   A. sinking down
   B. moving about
   C. carrying out
   D. helping to get

HINT: *This question asks you to identify the meaning of the word "maneuvering." Reread paragraph 10. Are there any clues to the word's meaning in the paragraph?*

7. The area where unusual things occur on the Great Lakes is called
   A. the Marysburgh Vortex.
   B. the Bermuda Triangle.
   C. the Straits of Mackinac.
   D. the St. Lawrence Seaway.

HINT: *This question asks you to recall a detail from the passage. If you are unsure of the answer, reread paragraph 10.*

8. What probably makes sailing the Great Lakes easier today?
   A. better captains
   B. smaller storms
   C. new technology
   D fewer freighters

HINT: *This question asks you to make a judgment based on the passage. If you're unsure of the answer, reread the end of the passage.*

9. Why did the author most likely write this passage?
   A. to explain why captains use the Great Lakes
   B. to describe the mysteries of the Great Lakes
   C. to discuss the importance of the Great Lakes
   D. to show the best way to travel the Great Lakes

HINT: *This question asks you to consider the author's purpose. Think about what you have read. Why do you think the author wrote this passage?*

10. The author says, "Surviving a Great Lakes storm is still a challenge, even with today's technology."
    • Besides storms, some of which appear suddenly, what are other factors that might account for missing ships? Explain.
    Use specific information from the article and any additional insight to support your response.

11. **Sailing on the Great Lakes has been compared to traveling in the Bermuda Triangle. For years, people have reported mysterious occurrences and unexplained happenings in both places. However, the U.S. Navy and the U.S. Coast Guard have stated that these occurrences are mainly caused by weather or human error.**

   • **Do you think that there are logical explanations for the mysterious happenings reported in these areas? Explain.**

   • **Do you think that mysteries do exist in human life? Explain.**

   Use specific information from the article and any additional insight to support your response.

YOU TRY IT

DIRECTIONS **INTRODUCTION**	Read this story/passage and answer the questions that follow. This passage tells about a little-known mystery that occurred over the American skies in the late 1800s. For the first time, an unidentified flying object was seen by many people over a period of months.

The First UFO

In November 1896, people began to report seeing a strange thing in the night skies. These reports continued for six straight months. Over 10,000 Americans saw an unusual object flying in the sky during the winter of 1896–1897.

Figure 1

People reported what they saw and described the object as being "oval" or "cigar-shaped with wings." A basket or long rectangle was said to be hanging under the oval. All reported seeing a bright light shining down toward Earth. Today, UFO experts claim that this "airship," or dirigible, was actually a ship from outer space. Interestingly, not one person in 1896 mentioned that it might have come from outer space.

The first reported sighting of the strange object was on November 17, 1896, in Sacramento, California. The sky was cloudy and rain was falling steadily. People who were out that night reported that a bright light suddenly appeared in the dark sky. It traveled slowly across the sky about a thousand feet above the rooftops of the town. Many people said that they saw a dark, oblong shape above the lights. *Figure 1* shows an artist's rendering of what the ship looked like. Then, the object simply disappeared.

The newspaper stories the next day called the thing in the sky an "airship." Some people thought it was a hoax. Playing practical jokes on others was a common pastime in the late 1890s. Even newspapers would print stories that were not true just to get people excited. As the days passed and no other sightings occurred, many people agreed that the sightings were a hoax.

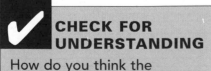

CHECK FOR UNDERSTANDING

How do you think the scientists were able to determine what the object in the sky was?

However, on November 22nd, the mysterious airship returned. Over the next few nights, the airship was seen all over the west coast. People in California, Oregon, and Washington saw the airship's lights in the night sky.

The people's excitement grew with each newspaper report of the sightings. Some reports said that the airship was the work of a mysterious inventor. Balloons had carried people for many years. In France in 1885, a dirigible flew a short, circular course. A model of a lighter-than-air vehicle was also being built in Germany. In 1885, Frederick Marriott built a model of an airship in San Francisco. His model was similar to the mysterious airship seen in the night sky. As of 1896, however, Marriott had not built a manned version of his airship.

6

By the beginning of December, the strange airship was no longer seen. Again, people thought that it had gone. Then, in January, the sightings began to occur in the middle of the country. Reports of the airship poured in from Nebraska, Kansas, Illinois, Indiana, and Texas. During the week of April 9–16th, over 110 reports were recorded. By the end of June, reports of the strange airship had all but stopped. It was never seen again. *Figure 2* shows the states in which the airship sightings were reported.

Explanations

Explaining something of this nature is difficult. It occurred over a hundred years ago. While there was only one photo of the machine, hundreds of people claimed to have seen it. Nonetheless, no real hysteria occurred because of the sightings.

The airplane would not be invented for another six years. The dirigible was being discussed as a way to fly. However, no working model of a powered one had yet been built. Therefore, it could not have been an airplane or a dirigible flying in the night skies.

There were some strange stories related to this incident. Some people said they had met with crew members. Others reported having seen the airship crash. These claims were never proven. Most people felt that they were not true.

Figure 2

Many experts feel that the planet Venus caused the sightings. During the time the airship was visible, Venus could be seen in the evening sky. Many of the reports were on cloudy or rainy nights. Venus was very bright in the sky at this time. Experts believe that people, when they looked into the night sky, were seeing Venus moving.

However, no one knows for sure what was seen in the night skies during the winter of 1896–1897. People saw and reported their sightings. Nobody can completely explain what it actually was that people saw in the night sky. Maybe it was, in fact, an unidentified flying object from outer space. ■

1. **People thought that the UFO was shaped like**

   A. a basket.

   B. a cloud.

   C. an oval.

   D. an oblong.

   HINT: *This question asks you to recall a detail from the passage. If you are unsure of the answer, reread the second paragraph.*

2. **Where was the UFO first seen?**

   A. Washington

   B. California

   C. Indiana

   D. Oregon

   HINT: *This question asks you to recall a detail from the passage. If you are unsure of the answer, reread the third paragraph.*

3. **Why didn't people think that the UFO might have been an airplane?**

   A. Airplanes had not been invented yet.

   B. Airplanes were not used in America.

   C. Airplanes were not flown during the night.

   D. Airplanes did not have any lights attached.

   HINT: *This question asks you to think about information from the passage. If you are unsure of the answer, skim-read the "Explanations" part of the passage.*

4. **Why didn't people always believe the stories they read in the newspaper?**

   A. Newspapers made many stories seem less interesting.

   B. Newspapers only printed stories by famous authors.

   C. Newspapers only offered the opinion of one person.

   D. Newspapers often made up stories to get people excited.

   HINT: *This question asks you to make a judgment based on information from the passage. If you are unsure of the answer, reread paragraph 4.*

5. In paragraph 6, the word "version" means
   A. photograph.
   B. event.
   C. model.
   D. court.

HINT: This question asks you to identify the meaning of the word "version." Reread paragraph 6. Are there any clues to the word's meaning in the paragraph?

6. What did *most* of the UFO sightings have in common?
   A. Most of the people met the UFO's crew.
   B. Most of the people heard strange sounds.
   C. Most of the reports were on rainy nights.
   D. Most of the reports were in large cities.

HINT: This question asks you to think about information from the passage. If you are unsure of the answer, reread the Explanations section of the passage.

7. Which of the following makes it most difficult to explain the sightings today?
   A. The sightings were not reported to the local police.
   B. The sightings happened over a hundred years ago.
   C. The people that made the reports were not trustworthy.
   D. The people who saw the "airship" waited to report it.

HINT: This question asks you to think about information from the passage. What about the people's stories might explain why it's difficult to explain them today?

8. What do some experts believe that people were seeing?
   A. the planet Venus
   B. a weather balloon
   C. lightning from a storm
   D. the reflection of light

HINT: This question asks you to recall a detail from the passage. If you are unsure of the answer, reread the end of the passage.

9. The author most likely included the map to
   A. identify places where airplanes were being used.
   B. point out places where airplanes were invented.
   C. show readers where people reported sightings.
   D. explain why only certain areas reported sightings.

HINT: *This question asks you to think about why the author included something in the text. Look back at the map. How did it affect the way you read this passage?*

10. Why did the author most likely write this passage?
   A. to describe what UFOs look like from the ground
   B. to show how reports of UFOs can be explained
   C. to explain why reports of UFOs have increased
   D. to tell readers about reports of the first UFO

HINT: *This question asks you to identify the author's purpose. Think about what you have read. Why do you think the author wrote this passage?*

11. **Practical jokes, even ones printed with all seriousness in the newspapers, were not unusual near the end of the 19th century.**
    - **Imagine that you were living at that time, and that you had heard and read the news about an unidentified flying object seen in your state.**
    - **How would you have reacted if the object had actually landed in your backyard? Explain.**

    Use specific information from the article and any additional insight to support your response.

12. **Throughout history, humans have constantly tried to extend the boundaries of their knowledge and experience, and these aspirations continue today. New discoveries in unexplored or little-known science and technology help to stretch these boundaries even more.**

   • **What connection can be made between people's reactions to the UFO sightings of more than a hundred years ago and how people have reacted to the news of space travel in recent history? Explain.**

   Use specific information from the article and any additional insight to support your response.

YOU TRY IT

The True Story of Sacajawea

Sacajawea was one of the greatest women of the west. She played a large role in making the Lewis and Clark expedition a success. Sacajawea was a guide, an interpreter, a diplomat, and a peace symbol. Yet, she was only 16 years old when she joined the expedition.

Initially, the expedition hired Sacajawea's husband, Toussaint Charbonneau, to be a translator. Lewis and Clark were spending the winter at the Fort Mandan Trading Post in present-day North Dakota. Charbonneau was a French-Canadian explorer and trader. He spoke both the Sioux and French languages. Lewis and Clark felt that he would help them talk with the many American Indian tribes they would meet.

While talking with Charbonneau, they learned that one of his wives was from the Shoshone tribe. Sacajawea, the daughter of a Shoshone chief, had been captured by an enemy tribe as a young girl. Charbonneau had won her in a game of chance.

Lewis and Clark asked Charbonneau to bring Sacajawea along with him because she spoke the Shoshone language and could interpret for them while on the trip. They also felt that having a woman along would send a message of peace to the other tribes because women never traveled with a war party. Charbonneau agreed to bring her even though she was pregnant with her first child at the time. The expedition left Fort Mandan in the spring. After giving birth to her son, Jean Baptiste, Sacajawea

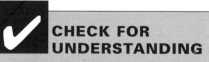
CHECK FOR UNDERSTANDING
Why do you think Lewis and Clark invited Sacajawea to join them on their journey?

carried him in a cradleboard on her back. Lewis and Clark realized that the new baby would add even more to the peaceful intent of the expedition.

5 When the expedition left Fort Mandan, no one realized the major role Sacajawea would play. Every day, she trudged along beside her husband. When they camped, she collected wood and cooked. It was not until several weeks later that the true nature of Sacajawea began to emerge. To begin with, she saved the expedition's logs, instruments, medicines, and trade goods from being lost forever. When a strong gust of wind capsized one of their boats, Sacajawea quickly jumped into the water and saved these important items.

When the expedition was near the place where Sacajawea had lived as a young girl, she began to tell them which trails to follow. Then Sacajawea became very ill. Several days passed and she did not recover. Still, her husband had her performing all her earlier jobs. Because his tent was larger and drier than hers, Lewis kindly moved Sacajawea to his tent to give her time to get well.

7 It was at this point that Lewis and Clark began to realize Sacajawea's true value to the expedition. Without her advice, it was more difficult to choose the correct trails. Her help would also be needed to translate when they met the Shoshone. Sacajawea would also be very useful in getting the horses needed to travel over the Rocky Mountains. She was crucial to the success of the expedition.

Sacajawea did recover. She assumed her role as guide and advisor to the group. In July 1805, she helped to save a number of the men who were caught in a flash flood. On August 17th, the expedition saw several Shoshone riding toward them. As they approached, Sacajawea realized that they were from her original tribe. She also saw that the chief was her older brother.

Lewis and Clark spent a week negotiating for the sale of horses. The Shoshone did not want them to have the animals. They were afraid that this would encourage other white men to come to their lands. Sacajawea intervened and the Shoshone sold them a number of horses; the expedition was thereby able to cross over the mountains.

The expedition finally reached the Pacific coast in the fall of 1805. They spent the winter in camp and returned to St. Louis the next year. When they traveled through the

Shoshone area, Sacajawea chose not to stay with her own tribe. She continued with the expedition. Later, she and her family left the expedition at an American Indian village along the upper Missouri.

From this point on, the historical records become clouded. At Clark's urging, Charbonneau eventually traveled to St. Louis. Clark hoped that Charbonneau and his son would like city life. It is assumed that Sacajawea went with her husband. However, Charbonneau did not stay in St. Louis. He returned to the west and worked for the American Fur Company. Sacajawea was assumed to have gone with him then as well. Their son, however, remained under Clark's care in St. Louis. **11**

Six years after the expedition, Sacajawea gave birth to a daughter. She named her Lizette. Sacajawea died in an epidemic of putrid fever late in 1812. She was only 24 or 25 years old at the time of her death. While some people think she lived to be 74 years of age and died in 1884, this is incorrect.

Sacajawea monument in Idaho

Court records show that William Clark adopted both of Sacajawea's children in August 1813. These records clearly state that, at the time of the adoptions, Sacajawea was dead. Clark's original notes substantiate that her death occurred in 1812. He described the last known whereabouts for each person on the expedition and lists Sacajawea as dead.

Today, we recognize Sacajawea as a person who played a major role in the Louis and Clark expedition. She was instrumental in the completion of their trip through the western frontier. ■

U.S. gold dollar coin honoring Sacajawea

1. Where did Lewis and Clark first meet Sacajawea?
   A. North Dakota
   B. France
   C. St. Louis
   D. Missouri

HINT: This question asks you to recall a detail from the passage. If you are unsure of the answer, reread the second paragraph.

2. Sacajawea saved a group of men from
   A. a sinking boat.
   B. a bad illness.
   C. a flash flood.
   D. a wild animal.

HINT: This question also asks you to recall a detail. If you are unsure of the answer, reread the middle of the passage.

3. What does the word "emerge" mean in paragraph 5?
   A. form
   B. appear
   C. suffer
   D. twist

HINT: This question asks you to identify the meaning of the word "emerge." Reread paragraph 5. Are there any clues to the word's meaning in the paragraph?

4. Why was having a woman on the trip important to Lewis and Clark?
   A. A woman would be familiar with the hiking trails.
   B. Women were more skilled at hunting animals.
   C. Only women were interpreters during this time.
   D. A woman would show that they meant no harm.

HINT: This question asks you to pull information from the passage. Did the passage mention a particular reason why Lewis and Clark wanted to include Sacajawea?

5. The purpose of paragraph 7 is to
   A. show how important Sacajawea was to the trip.
   B. explain why Sacajawea wanted to stay at home.
   C. tell readers what happened to Sacajawea.
   D. show readers how Sacajawea was treated.

HINT: This question asks you to think about a particular paragraph from the passage. Reread paragraph 7. Why do you think the author included this paragraph?

6. What did Sacajawea's husband do for a living?

   A. He was an explorer.

   B. He was a trader.

   C. He was a diplomat.

   D. He was an advisor.

HINT: This question asks you to recall a detail from the passage. If you are unsure of the answer, reread the second paragraph.

7. Why were the Shoshone afraid to give Lewis and Clark horses?

   A. They were afraid that Lewis and Clark would cause the animals harm.

   B. They were afraid that other white men would try to steal their horses.

   C. They did not want Lewis and Clark to have an easy journey to the coast.

   D. They did not want to encourage more white men to come to their lands.

HINT: This question asks you to think about information from the passage. If you are unsure of the answer, reread the section of the passage that discusses the Shoshone.

8. In paragraph 11, the words, "From this point on, the historical records become clouded" mean that

   A. the truth was buried by a certain person's lies.

   B. the truth about what happened is unclear.

   C. the records have become too hard to read.

   D. the records were destroyed many years ago.

HINT: This question asks you to predict the meaning of a particular sentence. Reread paragraph 11. Are there any clues to the author's meaning within the paragraph?

9. This passage is mostly about

   A. Lewis and Clark's journey through the American west.

   B. Lewis and Clark's interaction with American Indians.

   C. Sacajawea's importance to the expedition's success.

   D. Sacajawea's marriage to Toussaint Charbonneau.

HINT: This question asks you to identify the central idea of the passage. Think about what you have read. What do you think this passage is ultimately about?

10. **On August 17, 1805, Captain William Clark wrote this in his journal:**

    "...I saw, at a distance, several [American] Indians on horseback coming toward me. The interpreter [Charbonneau] and squaw [Sacajawea], who were before me at some distance, danced for the joyful sight, and she made signs to me that they were her nation. As I approached nearer them, [I] discovered one of Captain Lewis's party with them dressed in their dress. They met me with great signs of joy."

    • **What do you imagine were Sacajawea's thoughts and feelings at the time of this meeting out on the western frontier? Explain.**

    Use specific information from the article and any additional insight to support your response.

11. **When Lewis and Clark hired Sacajawea's husband, Toussaint Charbonneau, to be a translator, she came along even though she was expecting her first baby.**
    - **What did the explorers expect of Sacajawea when she first joined the expedition? Explain.**
    - **Did Sacajawea go beyond the expectations of her companions with all she managed to do during the two years and four months they were all traveling together? Explain.**

    Use specific information from the article and any additional insight to support your response.

CHAPTER 2

Understanding Text
Vocabulary and a Purpose for Reading

LS.6.4: PARAPHRASING/RETELLING (VOCABULARY)
RSL.6.6, RSI.6.6: RECOGNITION OF A PURPOSE FOR READING

You have probably learned a lot from reading. As you develop reading skills, you will understand more of what you have read and why the author has written the text. While taking the Common Core Language Arts Test, you should pay close attention so you can quickly recognize new words within the text. You should then try to determine the meanings of these words by studying the **context clues**.

While thinking about what you are reading, you will probably develop an idea of why the author wrote the text. Knowing the **author's purpose** gives you a deeper understanding of the text's meaning. It could also give you a hint about why the author chose certain words.

YOU TRY IT

You are reading a story at home and come across a word that you are not familiar with. What do you do?
• Do you look the word up in a dictionary right away?
• Do you try to guess what the unfamiliar word means by rereading the paragraph?

When taking the test, you won't have the opportunity to use a dictionary to look up a new word. Therefore, your best strategy would be to use context clues to give you hints about the word's meaning.

LS.6.4: PARAPHRASING/RETELLING (VOCABULARY)

What are context clues?

The sentences, phrases, and words that are surrounding a new word are **context clues.**

To really understand what is being said or written, you have to know the context – the facts, the circumstances, the setting, the event, or even the tone of the situation.

For example, when a person says, "Check!", we have to know the context to really understand what the person is trying to communicate. It could be an expression of agreement or understanding. It could be a call in chess to warn one's opponent that his or her king is exposed to direct attack. It could be a request for the bill in a restaurant. There are also other meanings that would tell us something quite different.

The elements the author has included in a passage – facts, circumstances, setting, events, or even tone – can be helpful in determining what an unfamiliar word means, particularly if a word has more than one meaning, like the example shown above. Where and when the story takes place gives the reader a clue about why the author has chosen to use certain words.

Sometimes just reading the paragraph again and looking at the words around the new word will help you figure out what it means.

Read this sentence:

On Thanksgiving Day, the family gathers for a delicious *shonilorate* to celebrate the good things in life.

What is a *shonilorate*? *Shonilorate* is a made-up word. You can tell from the words "Thanksgiving" and "family gathers" – the context clues – that by *shonilorate* the author means a special **dinner** or **meal**.

Here's one for you to try:

In the Hayden Valley of Yellowstone National Park live such *turberiling* as bison, elk, moose, wolves, and coyotes.

What is *turberiling*? Write your guesses below.

Which words in the sentence gave you clues? Write your guesses below.

Could the same word have two meanings?

Did you ever come across a word whose meaning you thought you knew, but that did not make sense in the sentence? This could be the case if the word has **more than one meaning**. The same word could have even more than two meanings.

A dictionary would be the best place to find out which meaning of the word is being used in what you are reading. However, when taking a test, it is best for you to use what you know from the context clues in the sentence to determine what the word means.

LET'S TRY IT TOGETHER

DIRECTIONS   Read the story and together we will discuss the questions.

The Promise of Springtime

Marcy had been pestering her father about planting bulbs since the spring, and he had finally consented to let her plant some. She had been growing plants throughout the winter using grow-light bulbs, but now she also wanted her own outdoor flower bed.

Her dad had replied, "Sure, Marcy, if you plant them and take care of them, you can plant spring bulbs this fall. I'm too busy these days to add to my list of things to do, but it would be nice to have some color in the yard. You will have to put them in just before the ground really freezes up so that they'll have enough time to develop roots."

Marcy wasn't sure how to do this, so she asked her dad for advice. In the days that followed, dinner conversation consisted of detailed explanations about planting bulbs.

Marcy had chosen crocus and snowdrop bulbs; these were the earliest flowers to bloom each spring. Sometimes they even bloom while there is still snow on the ground. Dad had said that these would be good ones to start with.

One cool fall day, carrying a bulky mesh bag, a trowel, and a ruler, Marcy made her way across the yard. After she found the perfect spot to plant her flowers, she got busy with the trowel turning the dirt over. Then she got the ruler out so that she could measure the depth for each bulb and the space in between.

Marcy's garden plot was a yard square. In the space where she had prepared the earth, she dug four narrow trenches and carefully put the bulbs in. She alternated the rows – first a row of crocuses and then a row of snowdrops, and so forth. She also tried to mix the four colors of crocuses – white, lavender, deep purple, and bright yellow. When all the bulbs had been arranged in the trenches, Marcy carefully covered them all with soil, patted the dirt down, checked to make sure she hadn't missed anything, and went to get the watering can.

As Marcy watered her little garden, she smiled to herself and thought, *Now I really can't wait for springtime to come!* ■

---

1. What does the word "bulbs" mean in each of these sentences?

> Sure, Marcy, if you plant them and take care of them, you can plant spring **bulbs** this fall.

Let's look at the context clues around the word **bulbs**. In this sentence, the words *plant* and *spring* tell what and when Marcy wanted to do something with the bulbs. So **bulbs** in this sentence could mean "underground leaf buds capable of developing into new plants," telling about the spring flowers Marcy was hoping for.

> She had been growing plants throughout the winter using grow-light **bulbs**, but now she also wanted her own outdoor flower bed.

In this sentence, the words "grow-light *bulbs*" describes special *light bulbs* used to make sure that plants have the light they need to grow and stay healthy. So, in this sentence, bulbs means "glass globes surrounding the elements of electric lights."

2. What does the word "yard" mean in each of these sentences?

> I'm too busy these days to add to my list of things to do, but it would be nice to have some color in the **yard**.

In this sentence, the word **yard** is talking about the place where Marcy will make her flower bed. When you think of the word **yard,** the first definition that probably comes to mind is "an area, usually with grass, adjacent to a house." Based on the context clues, it's clear that this is surely the definition meant in this sentence.

> The whole area for Marcy's garden plot was a **yard** square.

In this sentence, there is a description of the size of the area where Marcy will plant flowers. The word **yard** is used to mean "a standard measure of length, equal to three feet, or 36 inches." A yard square, or a "square yard", is an area where both the length and the width measure three feet.

HOMOPHONES

There are some very simple words that can be confusing when reading and writing. Some of these words are homophones.

Homophones are words that sound alike but have different spellings and different uses.

Let's look at a set of homophones – **would** and **wood**. These are not difficult words but they are very often confused. Using them correctly when you write will show the reader that you are a careful writer. You will need to know about homophones on the Common Core test.

WOOD	WOULD
The word **wood** means "what trees are made of; lumber; a forest."	The word **would** is the past tense of "will." It is used to express intent, uncertainty, possibility, or a request.
Examples: • Stop and think of how many everyday things are made of **wood**. • She ran into the **woods** to find the perfect camping location	**Examples:** • If the temperature were higher, the water **would** evaporate. • **Would** you like to join us for dinner?

LET'S TRY IT TOGETHER

Here are some for you to try. For each sentence, put the correct word – **wood** or **would** – in the blank space.

1. Every evening after dinner, they _____ read aloud.

2. The neighbors use a _____ stove.

3. _____ you please turn off the lights?

4. Is the toy truck made out of _____ or plastic?

5. Barbara wants a kitchen table made of _____ .

RSL.6.6, RSI.6.6: RECOGNITION OF A PURPOSE FOR READING

You might not think about it, but during an ordinary school day, you probably read a lot. If you made a list of them all, you will see that you really do read a variety of things during just one day at school.

In one sentence, can you explain just why you read? Of course, you want to learn and do well in school, but what other reasons do you have for reading? To find information? Entertainment? All of these are your **purposes for reading**.

While each piece of writing has its own different style, they all have one thing in common – they were each written with a purpose. While you are reading, think about what the author is trying to say. This will help you to discover the author's purpose.

The **author's purpose** is the reason why an author has written a particular story or text.

The reasons authors write are to **inform**, to **persuade**, to **instruct** readers about how to make or do something, and to **entertain** their audiences. Once you discover the author's purpose for each piece of writing, you will better understand what you read.

Here are some examples:

Q Why would an author write a history of an Olympic sport?
A Authors of histories usually want to *inform* readers.

Q Why would an author write directions for knitting a sweater?
A Manuals and instructions are written to *teach* readers to do something.

Q Why would an author write a book full of funny short stories?
A The author was most likely trying to *entertain* readers.

Q Why would an author write about the need for volunteers at a local shelter?
A The author probably wanted to *persuade* readers to become volunteers.

When you are reading, remember to keep in mind what your purpose is and what the purpose of the author was.

LET'S TRY IT TOGETHER

DIRECTIONS   Read the passage and together we will discuss the questions.

Labor Day

The first Labor Day holiday was celebrated on Tuesday, September 5, 1882, in New York City. By 1885, Labor Day was being celebrated in many industrial centers of the country.

"Labor Day differs in every essential way from the other holidays of the year in any country," said Samuel Gompers, founder and longtime president of the American Federation of Labor.

Labor Day, the first Monday in September, was created because of the labor movement and is a special day dedicated to the social and economic achievements of American workers. It serves as a yearly national tribute to all workers for the contributions they have made to the strength, prosperity, and well-being of our country.

More than 125 years after the first Labor Day observance, who first proposed the holiday for workers remains a mystery. Some records show that Peter J. McGuire, general secretary of a labor union called the Brotherhood of Carpenters and Joiners and a cofounder of the American Federation of Labor, was first to suggest a day to honor those "who from rude nature have delved and carved all the grandeur we behold." However, Peter McGuire's place in Labor Day history has not gone unchallenged. Many others believe that Matthew Maguire, a machinist, not Peter McGuire, founded the holiday.

The vital force of labor has brought the United States closer to the realization of its traditional ideals of economic and political democracy. It is appropriate, therefore, that the people of the United States pay tribute on Labor Day to the creator of so much of the nation's strength, freedom, and leadership – the American worker. ■

What was the author's purpose for writing this article?

Was it to persuade readers to work harder so they will be prepared to celebrate the next Labor Day?
No, that is not the author's purpose. The author does not try to convince readers that they should work harder so they will be prepared to celebrate the next Labor Day.

Was it to explain to readers how to celebrate Labor Day?
No, that is also not the author's purpose. While the article gives information about Labor Day, it does not tell readers how to actually celebrate the holiday.

Was it to entertain readers with an interesting story about an unusual holiday?
No, that is still not the author's purpose. While the article does tell an interesting story, it does not seem that the author's intention was simply to entertain.

Was it to inform readers about Labor Day and how it became a national holiday?
Yes, that is the author's purpose. The article informs reader about Labor Day and tells some of the history of the holiday.

When you are reading, ask yourself why the author has written what you are reading. If you remember to ask yourself several times while reading the passage, you may more easily see the hints about the author's purpose. Then, when you are taking the ASK6 Language Arts Literacy Test, you will be prepared for questions about author's purpose.

YOU TRY IT

| **DIRECTIONS** **INTRODUCTION** | Read this story/passage and answer the questions that follow. Bessie Coleman was the first African-American female to receive a pilot's license. This passage tells how she rose above several obstacles to become a trailblazer for women. |

Bessie Coleman: The First Black Female Pilot

Bessie Coleman

Bessie Coleman was born into a large family in Texas on January 26, 1892. Her father worked as a sharecropper and the family did not have much money. Things were difficult and, as Bessie grew older, she was expected to work around the house and in the fields picking cotton.

Bessie began attending a one-room school for African-American children when she was six years old. From the beginning, Bessie showed an interest in learning. She excelled in math. She completed all eight grades in the one-room school and then went to an all-black college, Normal University in Oklahoma. Unfortunately, Bessie ran out of money after one semester and she returned to Texas. However, that did not stop her from trying to learn, she continued to read as many books she could find.

3 In 1915, her life took the first of three dramatic turns. She left Texas to live with her two brothers in Chicago. She was 23 years old at the time. She wanted a chance to achieve something grand in life. Bessie thought the big city of Chicago would be filled with opportunity.

In Chicago, Bessie worked in barbershops as a manicurist. Then, during World War I in 1917, her brothers joined the army and went to fight in France. When they returned, they told Bessie about French women learning to fly. This prompted Bessie to take her life in a new direction. She decided that she wanted to be a pilot. However, no flight school in the U.S. would accept her because she was African-American and female.

Coleman with her plane, around 1922

Bessie decided to go to France to become a pilot. She learned French in night school while she raised the money to pay for her trip to France. By November 1919 she reached her goal and sailed for France.

Two years later, Bessie became the first African-American woman to be given a pilot's license, which she received from the Fédération Aéronautique Internationale (FAI). Following that, she decided to take more advanced flight training. That year she returned to New York.

Bessie's life took yet another turn when she began to perform aerial stunts in flying shows across the United States. Bessie knew she would have to do something different to attract paying customers; therefore, she began dressing in a military-style uniform and using eloquent vocabulary to speak about her flying activities. She became one of the more popular pilots at the air shows. However, Bessie refused to perform in any air show unless the audiences were desegregated, meaning that people from all races were allowed to sit together. Despite her fame, Bessie wanted more than just recognition for her flying exploits. She wanted to start a flying school for African-American aviators.

> ✔ **CHECK FOR UNDERSTANDING**
> Based on the information in the passage, how would you describe Bessie?

In April 1926, Bessie arrived in Jacksonville, Florida. She was there to do another air show. However, before she could do the show, she had to test a new plane she had just bought. While test flying the plane with Bessie in the passenger's seat, her mechanic lost control of the aircraft. As it flipped over, Bessie fell from the open cockpit to her death. She had left her seatbelt unbuckled to allow her to move around the cockpit.

People all over the nation mourned her death. Only after her death, though, did people begin to give Bessie the recognition she truly deserved. An Aero Club was started in Los Angeles in 1929. The club trained African Americans to be pilots. Bessie's example has inspired many African Americans to fly.

Even today, Bessie continues to receive recognition. Books have been written about her exploits. Roads have been named for her. A stamp, recognizing her accomplishments in aviation, was commissioned in her honor by the United States Postal Service in 1995. Bessie Coleman was a pioneer who overcame many obstacles to achieve her goals and dreams. ■

Pilot Bessie Coleman, 24, of Chicago, the first female African American aviator in the world, receiving a bouquet from Captain Edison C. McVey.

Bessie Coleman, U.S. commemorative stamp, 1995

1. Where did Bessie Coleman grow up?

   A. France

   B. Texas

   C. Los Angeles

   D. Oklahoma

HINT: *This question asks you to recall a detail from the passage. If you are unsure of the answer, reread the first paragraph of the passage.*

2. The purpose of the second paragraph is to

   A. explain why Bessie Coleman wanted to attend flight school.

   B. describe the places Bessie Coleman visited during her travels.

   C. show readers that Bessie Coleman was interested in learning.

   D. tell readers about the types of airplanes Bessie Coleman flew.

HINT: *This question asks you to think about why the author wrote a specific paragraph. Reread paragraph 2. What do you think the author was trying to say?*

3. In paragraph 3, the word "dramatic" means

   A. troublesome.

   B. remarkable.

   C. graceful.

   D. hidden.

HINT: *This question asks you to identify the meaning of the word "dramatic." Reread paragraph 3. Are there any clues to the word's meaning in the paragraph?*

4. Why did Bessie Coleman move to Chicago?

   A. so she could be closer to her brothers

   B. so that she could attend flight school

   C. so she could discover new opportunities

   D. so she could attend a good university

HINT: *This question asks you to recall a detail from the passage. If you are unsure of the answer, reread paragraph 3.*

5. **Why did Bessie Coleman most likely dress in a military uniform when she performed?**
   A. so people would know that she had fought in World War I
   B. so people would not be able to tell that she was a woman
   C. so people would give her more respect during her air shows
   D. so people would not think she was like the other pilots

HINT: This question asks you to make a judgment based on the passage. If you are unsure of the answer, reread the last few paragraphs of the passage, where Bessie's performances are mentioned.

6. **What is a theme of "Bessie Coleman: The First Black Female Pilot"?**
   A. Never give up on your dreams.
   B. Always look before you leap.
   C. Always listen to good advice.
   D. Never roam too far from home.

HINT: This question asks you to identify the theme of the passage. Think about what you have read. Was there one idea that carried throughout the entire story? Which of the answer choices best fits that idea?

7. **Bessie Coleman's story shows how turning dreams into concrete goals can help them come true.**

    • **How did Coleman translate her dream into a goal? Explain.**

    • **What steps did she take to make her dream a reality? Explain.**

    Use specific information from the article and any additional insight to support your response.

8. Bessie Coleman worked very hard to pursue her goal, and she succeeded. Unfortunately, a tragic accident cut her life short.
   • If Bessie Coleman had gone on to live a very long life, what do you think she would have accomplished in the years following 1926? Explain.
   Use specific information from the article and any additional insight to support your response.

YOU TRY IT

DIRECTIONS **INTRODUCTION**	Read this story/passage and answer the questions that follow. During World War II, a special group of women pilots flew military planes on special assignment. This passage tells about their heroic service.

Women Air Force Service Pilots

At one time, women were not allowed to fly military planes, and only male pilots had been trained to fly planes in combat. However, World War II changed that. Some women even flew military planes from the factories where they were built to the Air Force bases.

In December 1941, Japan carried out a surprise attack on the United States by bombing U.S. ships in Pearl Harbor, Hawaii. Following this sneak attack, Congress declared war on both Japan and Germany, officially becoming involved in World War II.

While preparing for war, members of President Franklin D. Roosevelt's administration realized that more than 100,000 military pilots would be needed to fight both enemy countries. These pilots would be expected to fly both in combat and by ferrying new planes from factories to the air bases.

A number of women had learned to fly in the 1930s. Some of these women were very good pilots and had many hours of flying experience. Jacqueline "Jackie" Cochran rose from childhood poverty to become a pioneer in aviation. She was the first woman to fly in the Bendix Trophy Transcontinental Race in 1935, winning it in 1938. Nancy Harkness Love, an accomplished pilot, had logged over 1,200 flight hours and was qualified to fly planes of 600 horsepower by the fall of 1942. Having worked to assist a company in ferrying

✔ CHECK FOR UNDERSTANDING

What prompted the U.S. to become involved in World War II?

aircraft, Love had a vision for the ability of women pilots to serve their country during wartime.

5 Love and Cochran suggested that the military use female pilots for some of the flying duties the war would demand. The two pilots felt that their fellow women could help win the war by flying military planes to air bases, thereby freeing up hundreds of male pilots for overseas combat. Initially, the Army Air Forces rejected this idea. They felt that it was too radical and they didn't think that women could fly military planes. However, within a short time, the Army Air Forces were forced to reconsider. They did not have enough male pilots to handle all the flying tasks needed to win the war.

In September 1942, the Air Force formed the first women's squadron at New Castle, Delaware. Nancy Love was its commander. It was called the Women's Auxiliary Ferrying Squadron (WAFS). Each of the 25 female pilots in the unit had a commercial pilot's license. Also, they each had over a thousand or more hours of flying time. In this group were the most experienced young pilots – male or female – in the United States at the time. They called themselves "The Originals."

After just 30 days of training in the military way of flying, these women started ferrying planes. They took planes as they came out of the factories and flew them to wherever they were needed. The group was so successful that the government decided to form another similar group. Letters were sent to all the women who had earned pilot's licenses, asking them to join this new group. Many women volunteered to join; however, they were sent to flight school for 23 weeks because they had not had as much flying experience as the women in the original group.

This second unit was called the Women's Flying Training Detachment. Jackie Cochran became its commander. Eventually, over 25,000 women applied for flight training in this group. A total of 1,830 were accepted and, of that number, 1,074 received their wings.

The training the female pilots received was not exactly like that of the male pilots. The women spent more time studying cross-country flying because they would be doing this in order to ferry planes from the factories to the air bases. They were not taught gunnery and formation flying; it was felt that they had no need to learn combat skills.

In the summer of 1943, the two women pilot groups merged to form the Women Air Force Service Pilots (WASP). The duties of this new unit were also expanded. Ferrying of planes was still a major task of this group, and they began flying other types of missions as well. For example, the female pilots began towing the targets used in gunnery practice by soldiers. Other women undertook searchlight and tracking missions. They simulated strafing[1], laying down smoke, and test flying. Still others flew personnel to bases all over the United States. The women pilots began flying all types of military planes, including both fighters and bombers. Two WASP flew the B-29 Super Fortress and one flew the experimental YP-59.

The work the WASP did was dangerous. While all flying involves some risk, the very planes these women flew increased their chances of getting hurt. In the early days of the unit, these women often trained on obsolete aircraft. They were also asked to ferry planes they had never been trained to fly. Generally, no pilot flies a plane until he or she has been trained on it. In wartime, however, some rules are relaxed. In these cases, the women were learning how to fly the plane while flying it for the first time.

These women risked death and injury for over 780 days during the war. Even though the women were not in combat, 38 were still killed while flying. Many were injured as well; seven suffered serious injuries and 29 suffered minor injuries. | **12**

In 1944, the war in Europe ended. Even though the war with Japan was still going on, the American pilots in Europe began returning home. The availability of these men caused the end of the WASP organization. Men were now available to do the tasks that women had been doing. The WASP were disbanded on December 20, 1944. Most of the WASP went back to private lives. Some of them joined the Air Force Reserve. A few remained in the military and made it their career.

Interestingly, the pilots in the WASP were never in the armed services. They remained civil service employees. They did not receive the same pay or benefits as the male military pilots. In 1977, Congress finally granted veteran status and limited benefits to the 850 living WASP.

The Women Air Force Service Pilots of World War II were pioneers. They were the first American women to fly military planes. They paved the way for the female pilots of today who fly military planes in combat. ■

[1]**strafing** *the practice of attacking ground targets from low-flying aircraft*

1. In paragraph 5, the word "rejected" means

   A. expected.

   B. encouraged.

   C. abandoned.

   D. approached.

HINT: *This question asks you to identify the meaning of the word "rejected." Reread paragraph 5. Are there any clues to the word's meaning in the paragraph*

2. What did a woman need to join the Women's Auxiliary Ferrying Squadron?

   A. a military fighter airplane

   B. a history of military training

   C. a letter from the government

   D a commercial pilot's license

HINT: *This question asks you to recall a detail from the passage. If you are unsure of the answer, reread paragraph 6.*

3. Why did the Air Force reconsider the idea of women pilots?

   A. The male pilots did not have as much flying experience as the female pilots.

   B. They did not have enough male pilots to perform all the tasks needed.

   C. The female pilots would only fly missions that were considered to be safe.

   D. The female pilots would fly for Japan if the Air Force refused them again.

HINT: *This question asks you to recall information from the passage. Did the author mention the military's reason for allowing women to become Air Force pilots? If you are unsure, skim the beginning of the passage for clues.*

4. Why did the government decide to form another women's flying group?

   A. The first group was very successful.

   B. The first group attracted little attention.

   C. Many women were volunteering to help.

   D. Many women were looking for new jobs.

HINT: This question asks you to think about information from the passage. If you are unsure of the answer, reread paragraph 7.

5. How were the first and second groups of women pilots alike?

   A. Both groups of women had over a thousand hours of flying experience.

   B. Both groups of women had to complete 23 weeks of training.

   C. All of the women had earned their pilot's licenses before joining the group.

   D. All of the women received letters from the government asking them to join.

HINT: This question asks you to make a judgment based on the information in the passage. What were similarities between the two female pilot groups?

6. How was the training of female pilots "different" from the training of male pilots?

   A. Female pilots did not fly planes across the country.

   B. Female pilots were not trained for combat missions.

   C. Female pilots were only trained for tracking missions.

   D. Female pilots were only trained to assist male pilots.

HINT: This question asks you to make a judgment based on the information in the passage. To help you, first eliminate answers that do not make sense.

7. The purpose of paragraph 12 is to

   A. show why the WASP was not needed after the war.

   B. describe how women felt when they joined the WASP.

   C. tell why the WASP were not part of the armed services.

   D. explain that the WASP's work was very dangerous.

HINT: This question asks you to think about why the author wrote a specific paragraph. Reread paragraph 12. What do you think the author was trying to say?

8. **What did most of the WASP members do when the war in Europe ended?**
   A. made the military their careers
   B. joined the Air Force Reserve
   C. returned to their private lives
   D. fought in the war against Japan

   HINT: This question asks you to recall a detail from the passage. If you are unsure of the answer, reread the end of the passage.

9. **How did the government finally show its appreciation for the WASP?**
   A. WASP members were considered veterans.
   B. WASP members were given medals of honor.
   C. WASP members were paid for their work.
   D. WASP members were remembered in a book.

   HINT: This question asks you to recall a detail from the passage. If you are unsure of the answer, reread the end of the passage.

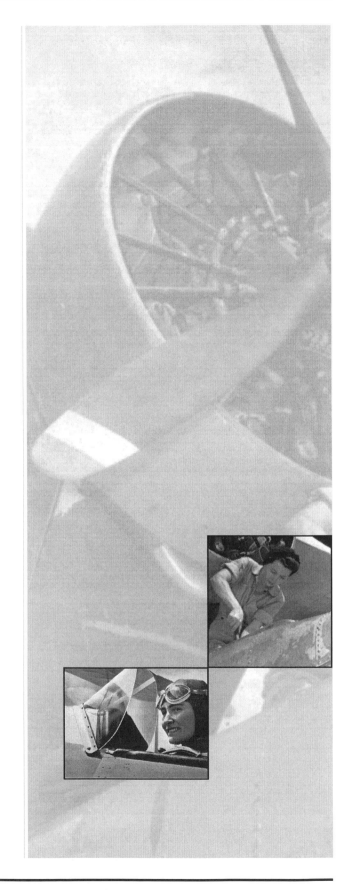

10. Trained and experienced female pilots were ready when the country needed their services during World War II.

   • Why was it so important for the first unit of Women Air Force Service Pilots to be successful? Explain.

   Use specific information from the article and any additional insight to support your response.

11. At first, the Air Force rejected the suggestion by Nancy Love and Jackie Cochran that they use women pilots because the idea was "too radical." However, the needs of a country at war led the military to accept women pilots only a short time after that.
    • Do you think that it was fair that the Women Air Force Service Pilots "did not receive the same pay or benefits as the male military pilots"? Explain.
    Use specific information from the article and any additional insight to support your response.

YOU TRY IT

DIRECTIONS
INTRODUCTION

Read this story/passage and answer the questions that follow. This is a story of an American Indian woman's struggles and triumphs in a land dominated by white men.

A Paiute Princess

Sarah Winnemucca Hopkins was the first American Indian woman to write a biography. In 1883, her book *Life Among the Paiutes: Their Wrongs and Claims* was published. She knew some unscrupulous Indian agents firsthand. Like other tribes, hers suffered from broken promises and the loss of their lands.

Sarah was born in a part of Mexico that was later to become the state of Nevada. Her father was the Southern Paiute Chief Winnemucca. She was named Thocmetony, meaning "shell flower."

Sarah Winnemucca Hopkins

Her grandfather, Truckee, had accompanied Captain John C. Fremont on his expedition across the Sierra Nevada Mountains to California in 1845. This trip made Truckee feel more friendly toward white people. In fact, his dying wish was that his granddaughter would be educated in a white people's school.

Unfortunately for the peaceful farming Southern Paiutes, some other tribes were more hostile. These tribes engaged in some skirmishes with white settlers. As a result, the government moved all of the tribes from the area onto a reservation in northern Nevada.

As a teenager, Thocmetony became a companion to a white girl. The girl's father worked for a stagecoach company. Thocmetony began adopting more of the ways of the whites. It was then that she took the name Sarah. Along the way, she learned English, Spanish, and several American Indian languages. Sarah, according to her grandfather's wishes, set off for the convent school in San Jose, California. She was 16 years old at the time.

It was while at the convent school that Sarah encountered prejudice. White families objected to having an American Indian student attending the school. So, within a matter of weeks, Sarah was forced to leave. She returned to her family.

7 In 1872, the U.S. government granted the Southern Paiutes land in Oregon. There, on the Malheur Reservation, they found fertile land to farm and a honest Indian agent. An Indian agent was an individual authorized by the U.S. government to supervise activities of Indian tribes. Their duties included distribution of government money to help tribes. Many agents were dishonest and corrupt. A responsible Indian agent named Samuel Parrish helped the Southern Paiutes. Sarah worked as his interpreter. All went well for a while until a bad agent named William Rinehart replaced him. Sarah went to the government to plead to have the agent removed. As a result, however, the agent banned her from returning to the reservation.

A few weeks later, Sarah learned of more trouble for her tribe. She was hired to guide three people from Oregon to Silver City, Idaho. Having made the trip several times, she was very familiar with this territory. This time was different, however; they found abandoned settlements with no signs of any settlers. At one of these sites, a cavalry troop rode up and warned them about an uprising of the Bannock tribe. Northern Paiutes from the Malheur Reservation had joined the Bannocks. All the settlers had gone to an army fort called Fort Lyon for protection. What distressed Sarah was learning that a Northern Paiute raiding party had kidnapped a large band of Southern Paiutes. Among those taken were her father and brother.

✔ **CHECK FOR UNDERSTANDING**

Why do you think Thocmetony's grandfather would have wanted her to attend "white people's school"?

Fort Lyon was under the command of General Oliver O. Howard. He knew that Winnemucca and his Paiutes didn't want to join the Bannocks in war. If they could gain their freedom, the army would offer them protection. Who would deliver this message to Winnemucca? Sarah was the logical choice.

The exact location of the Bannock camp was unknown. However, it was somewhere in the unmapped treacherous mountains of Idaho. To accomplish the task, 34-year-old Sarah faced enormous difficulties. Two scouts, John and George, accompanied her. In addition to starvation and death, the team had to worry about the general betraying them.

The three riders picked up the trail of the Bannocks along the Owyhee River. From time to time, they came across telltale signs as they climbed higher into the black granite mountains. They rode beside steep water-carved gorges, often a thousand feet deep. The horses had difficulty with their footing on the stony ledges.

Then, they spotted two men on a mountain slope. Drawing closer, Sarah saw that one of them was one of her brothers. He warned her of the hazards of trying to get a message to their father. There was only one unguarded, dangerous route into the camp. With this information, Sarah pressed on.

Donning her native dress, Sarah proceeded alone over the hazardous mountain trail to the Bannock camp. Under the cover of darkness, she sought out her father's tent. She persuaded him to gather the rest of their tribe and follow her to freedom.

On horses gathered by her brother and the scouts, the tribe raced for safety at Fort Lyon. However, the Bannocks, learning of the escape, pursued them. Sarah, with the two scouts and her sister-in-law, raced ahead to get help. She found the general at an outpost, and help was soon dispatched. Sarah had covered more than 200 miles in three days and two sleepless nights.

14

General Howard proved to be a man the Paiutes could trust. The location of the Bannock camp was now known. The general sent troops to put down the uprising. Later, he wrote a book, *Famous Indian Chiefs I Have Known*, in which he gave much praise to Sarah and to her efforts to help both the American Indians and the settlers live together in peace.

Sarah went on to teach, lecture, and work for American Indian causes. Despite several broken promises, the Southern Paiutes were eventually able to return to Malheur, Oregon. There they resumed their peaceful life as farmers. ■

1. Where was Thocmetony born?
   A. Oregon
   B. California
   C. Nevada
   D. Idaho

HINT: *This question asks you to recall a detail from the passage. If you are unsure of the answer, reread the beginning of the passage.*

2. Why did Thocmetony's grandfather trust white people?
   A. He had been helped by a group of white people.
   B. He had traveled with a group of white people.
   C. White people had left his tribe alone.
   D. White people had given his tribe land.

HINT: *This question asks you to think about the passage. Based on what you have read, what about Thocmetony's grandfather's history would have made him trust white people?*

3. Why did Thocmetony most likely change her name to Sarah?
   A. She thought the name sounded much prettier.
   B. Her grandfather had wanted her to change it.
   C. The name was more common among white people.
   D. She had to change her name to become a translator.

HINT: *This question asks you to make a judgment based on the passage. What do you think would motivate Thocmetony to change her name?*

4. Why did Sarah leave her school?
   A. She felt very lonely without her family.
   B. She didn't have enough money to stay.
   C. She wasn't doing well in her classes.
   D. She experienced prejudice at school.

HINT: *This question asks you to recall a detail from the passage. If you are unsure of the answer, reread the sixth paragraph.*

5. The purpose of paragraph 7 is to
   A. show why Sarah didn't trust white people.
   B. describe the many dangers that Sarah faced.
   C. explain why Sarah's grandfather sent her away.
   D. tell what Sarah thought about going to school.

HINT: *This question asks you to think about why the author wrote a specific paragraph. Reread paragraph 7. What did it tell you?*

6. Why did the settlers go to Fort Lyon?
   A. to find food
   B. to find water
   C. for their safety
   D. for their jobs

HINT: *This question asks you to recall a supporting detail from the passage. If you are unsure of the answer, reread paragraph 8.*

7. Why did Sarah want to find the Bannock camp?
   A. to rescue her family
   B. to escape from the Northern Paiutes
   C. to join their tribe
   D. to find a new companion

HINT: *This question asks you to think about information from the passage. If you are unsure of the answer, reread paragraph 8.*

8. In paragraph 14, the word "pursued" means
   A. scared.
   B. broke.
   C. stopped.
   D. chased.

HINT: *This question asks you to identify the meaning of the word "pursued." Reread paragraph 14. Are there any clues to the word's meaning in the paragraph?*

9. What did General Howard most likely think about Sarah?

   A. He thought that she was not
       trustworthy.

   B. He thought she was a very brave
       woman.

   C. He thought that she could be very
       rude.

   D. He thought she was not very
       cautious.

HINT: This question asks you to make a judgment about a character in the passage. Think about the interaction between Sarah and General Howard. Why did he choose her?

10. Why did the author most likely write this passage?

   A. to explain why General Howard
       could not be trusted

   B. to tell the story of a woman that
       made a difference

   C. to describe what life was like on the
       reservations

   D. to show why some tribes didn't get
       along well

HINT: This question asks you to identify the author's purpose. Think about what you have read. What do you think the author was trying to do?

11. Sarah Winnemucca earned the trust of her own people and praise from other significant leaders, such as General Oliver O. Howard.
   • What are some of the ways Sarah demonstrated that her tribe trusted her? Explain. Use specific information from the article and any additional insight to support your response.

12. The author states, "In addition to starvation and death, the team had to worry about the general betraying them."
    • Explain what the author means by this statement.
    • Describe what might have happened if the general had decided to betray the group.
    Use specific information from the article and any additional insight to support
    your response.

YOU TRY IT

DIRECTIONS INTRODUCTION	Read this story/passage and answer the questions that follow. Everyone knows about dolphins from television and from watching them in water park shows. However, few people know that the U.S. Navy has also trained dolphins for quite some time.

Navy Dolphins

Dolphins are intelligent sea mammals. Over the years, many have been trained to perform specialized tasks. These include finding things under water and jumping through hoops held high above the water.

Beginning in the 1960s, the U.S. Navy began to experiment with dolphins. The program was top secret; in fact, few people knew about it until the late 1980s. At that time, newspapers reported that dolphins were being used to find underwater mines during the Iran-Iraq War.

The navy had two goals when it started working with dolphins. One goal was to learn why dolphins are able to swim so fast and dive so deep. The navy wanted this information to help them design ships that moved faster in the water. They did learn enough to redesign the shape of some ships.

The second goal was to study how dolphins are able to find things under water. Dolphins possess the most sophisticated sonar known to man, called "echolocation." Dolphins can find things even under three feet of mud or in water so murky that humans cannot see more than a few inches into it. The navy wanted to train dolphins to find objects like mines and missiles without increasing the risk that they would explode. The "mine-sniffing" dolphins were taught to avoid touching the mines. If touched with enough force or pressure, the mines would explode. Instead, once a mine had been found, a dolphin would drop a weighted buoy line near the mine. Navy divers would then disarm it.

One dolphin was taught to carry mail and tools to an underwater lab. This dolphin repeatedly swam the 200 feet between the two locations. Not once did it lose anything it carried. This dolphin was also trained to guide lost divers to safety.

Dolphins have also been trained to guard ships. They were taught how to swim slowly around ships looking for swimmers and divers. If they spotted these uninvited guests, the dolphins would knock on a ball suspended from a patrol boat. Their handler would then know that an enemy swimmer was in the area. At the same time, the dolphins were taught never to attack a human swimmer. Navy dolphins

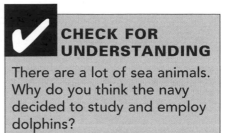

✔ CHECK FOR UNDERSTANDING

There are a lot of sea animals. Why do you think the navy decided to study and employ dolphins?

were also used to help guard the Republican Convention in 1996. These dolphins swam in San Diego Bay and helped provide security to the convention center located on the bay.

Dolphins have been used in war zones. They were used during the Vietnam War in 1970. They were used to detect enemy divers near ships. The second time was in 1987–1988. During the Iran-Iraq War, they were used to escort oil tankers through dangerous waters. Dolphins were also used in the 1991 Persian Gulf War. They were used to find mines in harbors. No dolphin was lost due to enemy action in any of these war zones.

The Russian Navy also trained dolphins. They started using dolphins in 1966 to provide security around their ships in the Black Sea. Russia also trained dolphins to find missiles and torpedoes that were fired during tests.

Both navies have used some dolphins in scientific research with sick children. Those children who stammer or who have cerebral palsy or autism improved faster when their therapy involved dolphins. The children were allowed to swim with the dolphins if they completed their therapy. Those children who received the same therapy without swimming with dolphins saw much less improvement in their conditions.

The U.S. Navy still uses dolphins. They are being trained to find mines in shallow water. The amount of noise in shallow water is much greater than in deeper water. The mechanical sonar that humans use does not work well in these areas. Dolphins can find mines and other objects much more easily.

It must be noted that the U.S. Navy's use of dolphins over the years has not been without controversy. The U.S. Navy insists that their marine mammals receive a standard of care that not only meets but goes beyond what is required by law, and that the animals are performing helpful services. However, opposition continues to come from animal rights' groups and from people who say that the gentle, intelligent animals are being trained for activities that go against their natures. ■

1. **Although "Navy Dolphins" is about the navy's use of dolphins, it would be useful background reading for an oral report on**
   A. visiting a water park.
   B. working at an aquarium.
   C. how to train dolphins.
   D. where most dolphins live.

HINT: *This question asks you to think about the information in the passage. Look at your answer options, Which one do you think would be best related to the topics in this passage?*

2. **In which of these wars did the navy use dolphins?**
   A. World War II
   B. Vietnam War
   C. Civil War
   D. Korean War

HINT: *This question asks you to recall a supporting detail from the passage. If you are unsure of the answer, reread the beginning of the passage.*

3. **What does the word "detect" mean in the following sentence from the article: "They were used to detect enemy divers near ships"?**
   A. find
   B. chase
   C. leave
   D. feed

HINT: *This question asks you to identify the meaning of the word "detect." Are there any clues to the word's meaning in the sentence?*

4. **What was the first task in which the navy used dolphins?**
   A. helping sick children finish therapy
   B. studying how to make ships faster
   C. looking for mines in shallow water
   D. guarding boats from enemy divers

HINT: *This question asks you to recall a supporting detail from the passage. If you are unsure of the answer, reread paragraph 3.*

5. What were dolphins trained to do when they saw an enemy swimmer?

   A. chase away the enemy swimmer

   B. search for new mines underwater

   C. touch a ball to alert their handler

   D. take a warning to an underwater lab

HINT: This question asks you to recall a supporting detail from the passage. If you are unsure of the answer, reread the middle of the passage.

6. How did people learn about the navy's dolphin program?

   A. The dolphins were seen in San Diego Bay at a political convention.

   B. Newspapers published stories about dolphins working during a war.

   C. The navy decided to show off its newly redesigned and faster boats.

   D. Dolphins began to carry mail and tools, and they guided lost divers.

HINT: This question asks you to recall a supporting detail from the passage. If you are unsure of the answer, reread the beginning of the passage.

7. The author of "Navy Dolphins" discusses the uses of dolphins by the navies of the United States and Russia.
   - In what ways does the author show that the uses of dolphins by the U.S. Navy and the Russian Navy are similar? Explain.
   - In what ways are they described as being different? Explain.

   Use specific information from the article and any additional insight to support your response.

8. According to the author, "Dolphins possess the most sophisticated sonar known to humankind, called 'echolocation.'"
   • How can you break down the word "echolocation" and use context clues to figure out what it is and how dolphins use it? Explain.
   Use specific information from the article and any additional insight to support your response.

YOU TRY IT

DIRECTIONS INTRODUCTION	Read this story/passage and answer the questions that follow. In September 1900, a powerful hurricane swept across the Gulf of Mexico and devastated the town of Galveston, Texas. It is recorded as the deadliest hurricane in U.S. history.

The Hurricane of 1900

On Friday, September 7, 1900, the people of Galveston, Texas were getting ready for Labor Day weekend. Two days later, almost every building in the town had been either damaged or completely destroyed.

In 1900, Galveston was an important cotton market. Cotton grown in Texas was shipped from Galveston all over the world. The city sits on the end of an island between Galveston Bay and the Gulf of Mexico. The island was about 30 miles long and from one to three miles wide.

The first hint of a storm appeared on Friday evening. Winds blowing at about 15 miles per hour started to rattle windows. By midnight, the winds had strengthened. However, the people were still not aware that a major hurricane was bearing down on their city. Storm-tracking equipment did not exist at that time. Instead, ships at sea would radio the position and the track of storms.

Unfortunately, many residents spent Saturday watching the heavy surf crashing onto the beach when they should have been making preparations to leave the island. By noon, the winds were gusting to over 50 miles per hour.

4

Around noontime, a ship tore loose from its moorings and destroyed the three bridges connecting Galveston to the mainland. With the major force of the hurricane only hours away, the 38,000 people in Galveston were cut off from safety.

No one seemed concerned, however. In their experience, the people of Galveston had survived other storms.

As evening approached, the winds became stronger. People started to realize that this was an unusually strong storm. The winds started to blow even harder, eventually reaching over 145 miles per hour. The rain fell so hard that it became impossible to see anything at all. By late Saturday, waters from the Gulf of Mexico had covered over most of the island.

7 Water flowed into homes all over the island. People were forced into their second and third stories to escape the water. Buildings all over the city started to collapse because of the surging water. The strong wind blew large pieces of wood all around. Many of the people running to higher ground were killed or maimed by this flying debris. By midnight, the water level was 20 feet above normal. The entire island was now under water.

By the early hours of Sunday, the storm had abated and the water had begun to recede from parts of the island. Even then, many of the residents were still forced to hold onto stationary objects to keep from drowning.

When daylight finally arrived in Galveston, people looked out on the worst devastation they had ever seen. One-third of the city had been obliterated. The buildings that were left had been badly damaged, and many of those still standing had to be torn down. The survivors stumbled around in a state of shock. Whole families had disappeared. In most families, at least one or more members were missing. Most sources agree that about 6,000 people died in Galveston and another 2,000 died along the Texas shore from this storm. Damage was estimated at $30 million in 1900 dollars.

The residents of Galveston started rebuilding as soon as the storm had passed. For safety reasons, they made two major changes to the city. The first was to build a 17-foot-high, three-mile-wide sea wall. The second was to increase the town's elevation to seven feet above sea level by dredging sand from the Gulf of Mexico.

As part of the rebuilding effort, material was pumped into the town to raise it's elevation.

Survivors set up temporary shelters in surplus U.S. Army tents along the shore. There were so many of them that observers began referring to this scene as the "White City on the Beach." Others constructed so-called "storm lumber" homes, using salvageable material from the debris to build shelters.

By September 12th, mail was received at Galveston for the first time since the storm. The next day, basic water service was restored, and Western Union began providing minimal telegraph service. Within three weeks, cotton was again being shipped out of the port.

Prior to the Hurricane of 1900, Galveston had been considered a beautiful, prestigious city. It was known as the "Ellis Island of the West" and the "Wall Street of the Southwest." However, after the storm, development shifted north to Houston, which had already begun to grow more prosperous.

Today, Galveston is a thriving port on the Gulf of Mexico. The safety improvements have worked. Hurricanes since 1900 have not caused nearly the loss of life and damage that the Hurricane of 1900 did. ■

1. **Though "The Hurricane of 1900" is about a hurricane that hit Galveston, Texas, it would be useful background reading for a report on**
   A. what happens when bridges are ruined.
   B. large disasters in U.S. history.
   C. how to report bad storms on the ocean.
   D. rebuilding a waterway after a storm.

HINT: This question asks you to think about the author's purpose. Think about what you have read. In what instance would someone researching a report need this information?

2. **What was the first sign of a storm approaching Galveston?**
   A. A boat destroyed three bridges from the island.
   B. People began getting ready for Labor Day.
   C. Winds began blowing on Friday evening.
   D. Water began to flood the first floors of homes.

HINT: This question asks you to think about information from the text. Where does the author first mention the storm approaching?

3. **What does the word "surging" mean in paragraph 7?**
   A. floating
   B. rising
   C. ocean
   D. dirty

HINT: This question asks you to identify the meaning of the word "surging." Reread paragraph 7. Are there any clues to the word's meaning in the paragraph?

4. **Why were people unprepared for the storm?**
   A. People were preparing for Labor Day weekend.
   B. A boat had destroyed the three escape bridges.
   C. Galveston was next to the Gulf of Mexico.
   D. There was no system of tracking storms.

HINT: This question asks you to think about information from the passage. Read the answer options. Which one best explains why the people were unprepared?

5. Why did the residents of Galveston build a 17-foot-high seawall?

   A. to keep the ocean level from reaching the city again

   B. to stop any other hurricanes that approach Galveston

   C. to keep sharks from the city while it is under water

   D. to stop debris from being washed back by the tide

HINT: This question asks you to make a judgment based on the passage. If you are unsure of the answer, reread the information pertaining to rebuilding after the storm.

6. Which of the following best describes how Galveston residents felt after the storm hit?

   A. grateful

   B. annoyed

   C. generous

   D. shocked

HINT: This question asks you to think about information from the passage. How did the author describe the reactions of the people of Galveston?

7. The purpose of paragraph 4 is to

   A. tell when the storm reached fifty miles per hour.

   B. describe what people did on the city's beaches.

   C. demonstrate what the city's residents should have done.

   D. explain how residents react to storm warnings now.

HINT: This question asks you to think about why the author wrote a particular paragraph. Reread paragraph 4. What do you think the author was trying to say?

8. Galveston residents were caught unaware by the Hurricane of 1900. However, steps have since been taken in the hope of preventing this level of destruction from happening again.

   • Explain how, if a hurricane were to threaten Galveston today, the residents might be better prepared than they were in 1900.

   Use specific information from the article and any additional insight to support your response.

9. Recently, Dr. Stephen P. Leatherman, director of the International Hurricane Research Center, released a list of the "10 Most Vulnerable U.S. Mainland Areas to Hurricanes." Galveston is #6 on the list and Long Island, New York, is #8.
   • Which questions do you think that people who live in or near the vulnerable areas should be asking their local and state government leaders about preparations for a hurricane? Explain.

   Use specific information from the article and any additional insight to support your response.

CHAPTER 3

Analyzing Text
Text Organization

RSL.6.5, RSI.6.5: RECOGNITION OF TEXT ORGANIZATION

Genres are different kinds of writing. Two genres you will see on the Common Core Language Arts Test are informational text and narrative text.

In **informational text**, the meaning is usually pretty straightforward. You are given information and/or you are given instructions about how to make or do something.

In **narrative text**, however, there can be layers of meaning. What the words on the page tell you directly is the **explicit meaning**. There may also be a "deeper" meaning. This may be an idea, a moral, or a truth that is suggested or implied by the text, but is not state directly. This is the **implicit meaning**.

YOU TRY IT

You have just finished reading a passage. Your teacher asks you why the author has included a particular chart. How can you find the answer?
• Do you go back and skim the passage?
• Do you think about what the passage was about?
• Do you compare the information in the chart to the central idea?

You should do all of the above. In order to determine the reason why a particular diagram or image is included, you should think about what the story is trying to communicate.

RSL.6.5, RSI.6.5: RECOGNITION OF TEXT ORGANIZATION

> ### How are texts organized?

Before you read a passage, can you tell just by looking at the title what kind of writing it might be? If you can, you will be a step ahead as you work your way toward completely understanding what you read.

Ask yourself these questions:
- What is the central idea of the story?
- How is the text organized?
- What is the style of the text?

TEXT ORGANIZATION   Each passage has three important parts. No matter how short or long a passage is, it has to have a **beginning**, a **middle**, and an **end**.

BEGINNING
The beginning of the passage is the first paragraph, paragraphs, or even pages, depending on the length of the passage. In this part of the passage, you will be introduced to the setting and the characters.
SETTING: the time, place, or location where the story takes place
CHARACTERS: the people in the passage

MIDDLE
The middle of the passage is the next paragraph, paragraphs, or pages, depending on the length of the passage. In the middle of the passage, you will learn about the plot.
PLOT: the action of the passage; when the story progresses

END
The end of the passage is the final paragraph, paragraphs, or pages, depending on the length of the passage. The end of the passage contains the conclusion.
CONCLUSION: how the passage wraps up the plot; how everything turns out

What are genres?

Genres are categories used to define types of writing.

You have probably read many different genres already, and you surely know about narrative text and informational text.

Some genres have **sub-genres** as well. A sub-genre can further explain what the story is about. Some sub-genres are science fiction, fantasy, and biography. For example, a science fiction story could be about space or some kind of futuristic world, but it will always fall under the heading of fiction.

GENRE: NARRATIVE TEXT

Narratives are stories that tell about one or more persons, experiences, or events.

Most narrative stories are usually told in the order in which things happened. Some of the many different kinds of stories are adventure stories, legends, myths, folk tales, fairy tales, and mystery stories.

The narrative body of writing called **fiction** is composed of made-up stories.

The narrative body of writing called **nonfiction** is composed of true or factual stories.

Sometimes fiction and nonfiction overlap, as they do in a story that is historical fiction. In a work of historical fiction, an author uses historical facts as the setting and the background for a story that may involve individual characters or events which have been made up.

GENRE: INFORMATIONAL TEXT

An author writes an **informational text** to tell readers how to do something or to give them information.

Depending on the topic or theme, informational texts sometimes have directions or steps. In order to understand an informational text of this kind, you have to look at the way it is organized. If it has steps, the steps are usually numbered (Step 1, Step 2…).

There may be pictures along with the steps to illustrate exactly how to do something. If there are pictures, look carefully at each picture and pay attention to how each one goes along with the text you are reading. You may have to answer questions about them.

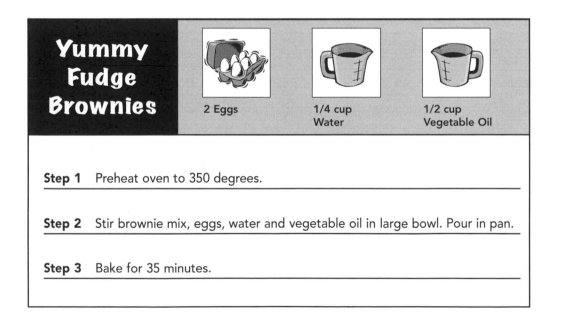

Yummy Fudge Brownies

2 Eggs 1/4 cup Water 1/2 cup Vegetable Oil

Step 1 Preheat oven to 350 degrees.

Step 2 Stir brownie mix, eggs, water and vegetable oil in large bowl. Pour in pan.

Step 3 Bake for 35 minutes.

LET'S TRY IT TOGETHER

DIRECTIONS   Read the passage and together we will discuss the questions.

People sometimes have to get in touch with organizations or businesses by mail. This is a more formal way of communicating than a letter to a friend would be. Read this example of a business letter.

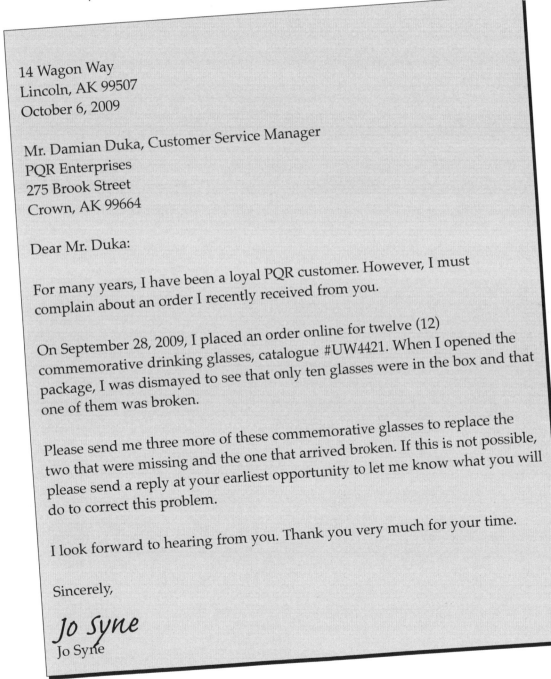

14 Wagon Way
Lincoln, AK 99507
October 6, 2009

Mr. Damian Duka, Customer Service Manager
PQR Enterprises
275 Brook Street
Crown, AK 99664

Dear Mr. Duka:

For many years, I have been a loyal PQR customer. However, I must complain about an order I recently received from you.

On September 28, 2009, I placed an order online for twelve (12) commemorative drinking glasses, catalogue #UW4421. When I opened the package, I was dismayed to see that only ten glasses were in the box and that one of them was broken.

Please send me three more of these commemorative glasses to replace the two that were missing and the one that arrived broken. If this is not possible, please send a reply at your earliest opportunity to let me know what you will do to correct this problem.

I look forward to hearing from you. Thank you very much for your time.

Sincerely,

Jo Syne
Jo Syne

After having written the letter, you must then send it off. Follow these steps to properly mail your letter off to the business or organization you're trying to reach.

HOW TO PREPARE A BUSINESS LETTER FOR MAILING	
Step 1 Sign the business letter with a pen in the space above the typed name.	**Step 4** Place first-class postage in the upper right-hand corner of the envelope.
Step 2 Carefully fold the letter into thirds.	**Step 5** Put the letter into the envelope and seal it.
Step 3 Write the address of the person you are sending the letter to in the center of the envelope. Write your address in the upper left-hand corner of the envelope.	**Step 6** Mail the letter promptly.

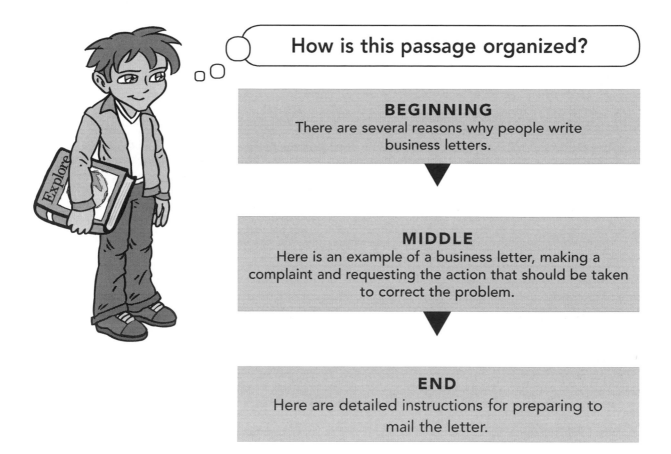

How is this passage organized?

BEGINNING
There are several reasons why people write business letters.

▼

MIDDLE
Here is an example of a business letter, making a complaint and requesting the action that should be taken to correct the problem.

▼

END
Here are detailed instructions for preparing to mail the letter.

What is the genre of this passage?

This is an example of informational text. How do we know? We have learned that, in informational text, the author is trying to inform the reader about how to do something or to give him or her information that will be useful in his or her everyday life.

This letter is an example of a business letter written by a dissatisfied customer. The customer expresses her complaint in detailed steps in this letter. She tells how she would like the situation to be resolved. Knowing how to write a business letter is a useful and practical skill. The steps that then follow show how to do something, a clear indication of an informational text.

FINDING MEANING IN TEXT

A lot of the narrative texts that you will read have both an explicit meaning and an implicit meaning. As you read, you probably pay attention to what the characters are saying. You should also look for meaning in the character's actions. The words you are reading don't always directly state what is happening.

What the words tell us is the **explicit meaning**; it is stated fully and clearly. The **implicit meaning** it is not expressed in words; it is implied.

You can find the implicit meaning by thinking about what the words are telling you. What does the story tell you about life? The implicit meaning may be the moral of the story.

THE ANT AND THE DOVE
An Ant went to the bank of a river to quench its thirst. Being carried away by the rush of the stream, it was on the point of drowning. A Dove, sitting on a tree limb overhanging the water, plucked a leaf and let it fall into the stream close to the Ant. The Ant then climbed onto it and floated safety to the nearby bank.

Shortly afterwards, a birdcatcher came and stood under the tree, and laid a trap for the Dove, which sat in the branches. The Ant, understanding the man's intent, stung him in the foot. The birdcatcher howled in pain and the noise scared the Dove out of the tree. ■

- The explicit meaning of this narrative text is that a dove saves an ant's life and then, in return, the ant saves the dove from being trapped.

- The implicit meaning, which you can think of as the moral of the story, is that one good turn deserves another. If you do nice things for people, they are likely to do nice things for you in return. Another implicit meaning could be that people sometimes do nice things for each other even when they don't have to or aren't expected to, just to serve their fellow man.

LET'S TRY IT TOGETHER

DIRECTIONS   Read the story and together we will discuss the questions.

The Skating Accident

Out on the ice on Friday evenings in winter, Chuck and his friends had lots of laughs; some of them would even try fancy moves, but always in good fun. In an effort to show off his abilities, Chuck flew over to one side of the pond. Wait till they see this, he thought, grinning to himself.

Chuck rapidly picked up speed, slicing into the ice and kicking his heels into the air with each stroke. In his mind, he was a professional speed skater, sailing along the ice at record-breaking speeds. Glancing ahead, Chuck suddenly caught a glimpse of the full moon through the tree branches. Wow! he thought. That is pretty incredible!

Before he knew what was happening, Chuck felt his right skate skid into a rough patch of ice. His blade collapsed under him and he fell with a thud to the pond's icy surface. He immediately heard a crack and knew that something had broken. He just hoped that it wasn't the ice!

Immediately, Chuck's friends were rushing to his side.

"What happened?" Marika cried, kneeling down beside him. "Are you OK, Chuck?"

"I think I'll be all right," Chuck replied, wincing as he tried to sit up. Pain shot up his right side.

"Maybe you'd better stay still, Chuck," Tyson said. "I'll call 911 and your parents. Seth, don't you have a blanket with you?"

Seth scurried off to find his blanket for Chuck, while Tyson hurriedly dialed the emergency numbers and clearly explained the situation into the phone.

As they waited for help to arrive, Jenn asked Chuck, "What were you trying to do?"

Chuck ducked his head and blushed. "I was trying to show off, I guess. That'll teach me to be paying more attention to style and speed than to safety!" ■

1. What is the explicit meaning of this story?

Is it that a group of friends went ice skating?
No, that is not the explicit meaning. The ice skating party is part of the setting for the story, and that is important. However, it does not tell us what the explicit meaning of the story is.

Is it that there was a full moon?
No, that is not the explicit meaning either. While the moon contributed to Chuck's fall, it is not the story's explicit meaning.

Is it that Chuck suffered an injury because he wasn't paying attention?
Yes, that is the explicit meaning of the story. The words of the story let us know that Chuck was injured while trying to impress his friends with is fancy skating.

2. What is the implicit meaning of this story?

Is it that Chuck and his friends have skated for years?
No, that is not the implicit meaning. In fact, the reader does not know for how long the kids have even known each other.

Is it that everyone knew what to do when Chuck fell down?
No, that is not the implicit meaning either. It is true that certain members of the group knew just what they should do for a person who has just fallen, but that is not the implicit meaning of the story.

Is it that a person should focus on more important things than how they look?
Yes, that is one possible implicit meaning of the story. Chuck was trying to show off, which is not a very good way to act, by impressing his friends with his speed and skating style. Unfortunately, he managed to injure himself instead. At the end of the story, Chuck has learned a valuable lesson about taking something too far and becoming showy or boastful.

YOU TRY IT

Dolley Madison

Dolley Madison was one of the most important women of her time. For most of her adult life, she was a famous hostess and fashion trendsetter. She also had a great impact on political decisions. She spent 16 years in and around the White House in Washington. Dolley was also a genuine war hero who saved many important documents from being lost during the War of 1812.

Dorothea Dandridge Payne, nicknamed Dolley, was born in 1768 in North Carolina while her family was visiting her grandparents. Her Quaker family lived in Virginia, and most of Dolley's early life was spent on a plantation in that state. While growing up, Dolley preferred to play with her six brothers and their friends. She would go on fishing trips, ride horses, and shoot guns. Her mother punished her for this tomboyish behavior; yet, Dolley did not stop playing with her brothers.

In July 1783, Dolley's father John Payne freed his slaves and moved the family to Philadelphia to give the children a better education and to help them be closer to their Quaker roots. Dolley was 15 years old at the time. Within a few years, her father's business failed. Dolley was forced to leave her Quaker school and help around the house. She was a good cook and tried to maintain a sense of humor during the difficult times her family experienced. She married John Todd, Jr. in 1790 and had two sons. Sadly, her husband and one son died of yellow fever just three years later.

3

Dolley moved back to her parents' home after her husband's death. Her father and mother had been reduced to renting out rooms to make ends meet. Dolley once again helped with the cooking and cleaning. In the evenings, she would socialize with the boarders. At this time, Dolley began to show an interest in politics. It was not unusual for her to voice her own ideas on the issues being discussed.

5 Within a year, Dolley had married James Madison. He was a representative from Virginia and 17 years older than her. Following her marriage, she left the Quaker faith and discarded their somber dress style. She started wearing the finest fashions.

The Madisons moved to Washington, D.C., when it became the nation's capital. Their home became the center of society in the new town. When Thomas Jefferson was president, Dolley often served as hostess in the White House. When her husband became the fourth U.S. president in 1809, Dolley continued in her role as hostess. She was beautiful and gracious, and nearly everyone loved her.

As first lady, Dolley was the hostess at the nation's first inaugural ball. She held weekly public social meetings at the White House. Dolley also met with the wives of government officials on a regular basis. She was known for voicing strong opinions. Her husband often sought her advice on the issues facing the country. Other people sought her wise counsel, too. Dolley also liked to go to horse races and to gamble at cards.

✔ **CHECK FOR UNDERSTANDING**

Why do you think the author goes into so much detail about Dolley Madison's childhood?

Dolley was the first to institute a number of activities that still go on today at the White House. For instance, she started the children's Easter Egg Roll. She also began the custom of planting trees on the White House lawn. She was the first wife to watch her husband take the oath of office. Dolley also got women to watch from the gallery as Congress passed laws. Before this, only men had done so. In fact, she was the only person – and a woman at that! – allowed to sit in on Congress, on the congressional floor, while it was in session.

During the War of 1812, Dolley became a war hero. The British Army attacked Washington, D.C. in 1814. Dolley was responsible for saving many American documents from being burned. She also managed to save a Gilbert Stuart painting of President George Washington. Since she could not simply pull it off the wall because the frame was screwed to it, she had a caretaker cut the painting out of the frame. When the

 Explore CCSS/PARCC Grade 6 Reading

ordeal was over, Dolley then helped to organize the rebuilding of the White House.

At the end of James Madison's second term as president, Dolley and her husband returned to Virginia. However, following her husband's death in 1836, Dolley once again returned to Washington, D.C. She moved into a house across the street from the White House. Overnight, she became a celebrity. People invited her to all the local social events.

Unfortunately, the last years of Dolley's life were not easy. Near the end, she had little money. Her son had lost the family fortune. She was forced to sell her husband's papers and their house in Virginia to friends. Even with this money, Dolley had to live frugally. She died in 1849 at the age of 81. Today, we remember Dolley Madison as one of the best-loved, most remarkable first ladies ever to have lived in the White House. ■

1. The purpose of the third paragraph is to

  A. explain why Dolley's family left Virginia.

  B. describe the difficult times that Dolley faced.

  C. tell readers about Dolley's tomboyish nature.

  D. show readers why Dolley was loved by many.

HINT: This question asks you to identify why the author wrote a particular paragraph. Reread paragraph 3. What is the author trying to say?

2. Why was Dolley Madison forced to leave her school?

  A. They told her to give up riding horses.

  B. They did not like the way she dressed.

  C. She did not practice the Quaker faith.

  D. She had to help out around the house.

HINT: This question asks you to recall a supporting detail from the passage. If you are unsure of the answer, reread paragraph 3.

3. What does the word "discarded" mean in paragraph 5?

  A. updated

  B. abandoned

  C. designed

  D. exhibited

HINT: This question asks you to identify the meaning of the word "discarded." Reread paragraph 5. Are there any clues to the word's meaning in the paragraph?

4. Dolley Madison encouraged other women to

  A. voice their political opinions.

  B. plant trees in their yards.

  C. watch Congress pass laws.

  D. host parties at their homes.

HINT: This question asks you to recall a detail from the passage. If you are unsure of the answer, reread the eighth paragraph.

5. Why was Dolley Madison considered a war hero?

   A. She rescued documents and a painting from destruction.

   B. She saved the White House from being burned down.

   C. She warned people that the British army would attack.

   D. She fought against the British army with her husband.

HINT: Based on what you have read in the passage, which of the answer options best describes why Dolley Madison may be called a war hero?

6. Why did the author most likely write this passage?

   A. to tell readers about the clothes Dolley Madison wore

   B. to describe how Dolley Madison dealt with difficult experiences

   C. to show readers what made Dolley Madison so popular

   D. to explain why Dolley Madison was an important part of history

HINT: This question asks you to think about why the author wrote this passage. Think about what you have read. What do you think the author was trying to say?

7. "Dolley Madison" tells the story of this First Lady from her birth in 1768 to her death in 1849.
   • How would you describe the way this text is organized? Explain.
   • Why is this pattern suitable for biographical accounts? Explain.
   Use specific information from the article and any additional insight to support your response.

8. Plainness in dress and in speech – an important part of the Quaker lifestyle – is based on the principles of simplicity, equality, and integrity.
   • What did Dolley Madison do during her lifetime to uphold Quaker principles? Explain. Use specific information from the article and any additional insight to support your response.

YOU TRY IT

DIRECTIONS **INTRODUCTION**	Read this story/passage and answer the questions that follow. Have you ever set off for a very nice evening only to have your plans unexpectedly change? This is that kind of a story. Read what happened to a couple after they spent a rather rocky evening in the city.

Accidents Happen

It was 3:30 in the morning. The temperature was moving closer to freezing, but the wind chill made it feel even colder. Terri was warming her numb fingers around a steaming mug of coffee. She was shivering, but it wasn't just from the cold. The past hour and a half had a lot to do with her emotional state.

Jacques, her husband, sat alongside her at the counter of an all-night diner. For now, he seemed calm and in control of his emotions. However, he knew that once the adrenaline wore off, his feelings would change as he relived their close call.

Cold and shaken by their experience, they had gladly entered the welcoming warmth of the diner. It had been a night neither were unlikely to forget! It all started sometime shortly before midnight....

Jacques and Terri had gone to their car to drive back home to Middletown, New Jersey. They had met friends for dinner and a show in New York City. Afterwards, when they got to where they had parked their car, it was missing. Immediately, they thought it had been stolen. They called the police, only to learn that their car, along with several others, had been towed away. It seems they had mistakenly parked in a tow-away zone. Unfortunately, Jacques had not seen the sign at the far end of the street when he had parked the car. The policewoman they spoke to informed them that they would have to wait until morning to pay their fine and retrieve the car from the city impound lot.

"Oh, what an annoyance," Terri cried. "I mean, we were only inside for about two hours. The least they could've done was make an announcement or something."

"Still, Terri," said Jacques, "it was irresponsible of me to have parked there. Accidents happen, I guess, but if I had known we were parked illegally, I certainly would've found another spot."

> ✔ **CHECK FOR UNDERSTANDING**
>
> What do you think could have happened to leave Jacques and Terri "cold and shaken?"

"I guess so," Terri replied, "but who needs this on a night like tonight? It's freezing out here!"

"Well, in a busy city like New York, I can't blame them for treating this like any other routine traffic violation. They're just doing what they're supposed to do."

Terri, who was in a foul mood after having disliked the food she had ordered at the restaurant and having been disappointed by the show they had chosen to see, wasn't convinced. "Well, bad things always happen in threes, they say, and this just about rounds out a perfect evening," she said sarcastically. "Things certainly can't get much worse."

Neither Jacques nor Terri wanted to remain in the city overnight, so they called a local rental company, who delivered a rental car right to where they were waiting, shivering in the chill air. As they drove home, the couple tried to come up with a plan to get their car back.

"I suppose I could call into my office in the morning and explain the situation to them," Jacques said. "I'll just tell them I'll be arriving by mid-morning."

"Sounds good to me, if you don't mind the extra hassle and your boss doesn't mind the missed work," Terri replied, finally allowing her bad mood to dissolve and settling back into her seat.

"I'll only be a few hours late, I would think, and I'll make up the time, too. That way, I can return the rental car and hop on the subway to go get our car from the impound lot." Unfortunately, Jacques had no idea that this would be a much more complex task than he was anticipating.

Just moments later, as they rounded a bend in the dark highway, a large object appeared directly in their path. A mattress had apparently fallen off another vehicle and had landed in the center of the roadway.

Jacques had no time to swerve into another lane to avoid it. He maneuvered the car haphazardly, hoping that he might drive in such a way as to pass the mattress between the wheels. No such luck – they plowed right into it!

The mattress somehow attached itself to the undercarriage of the car, making it so that Jacques and Terri were now dragging it down the highway. As Jacques began slowing down, he and Terri began to smell smoke. The heat from the car's exhaust and the friction dragging the mattress along the pavement had caused it to catch on fire.

"Get out of the car, Terri!" Jacques exclaimed.

"I'm going!" Terri cried, snatching her purse as she and Jacques leaped from the car as soon as it came to a complete stop.

The couple quickly scrambled for the emergency lane in case another vehicle happened to come around the corner. They had to put distance between themselves and the automobile as the flames moved dangerously close to the gas tank. Jacques grabbed Terri's arm and pulled her along, making her wish she hadn't been wearing high heels.

Luckily, a passing motorist saw the danger and used his cell phone to call 911. Nonetheless, by the time help arrived, the car and the paperwork that went along with it were total losses. It took a long time for Terri and Jacques to explain to the police what had happened and to complete the accident report. It took considerably longer to explain the loss of the automobile to the frantic night manager of the car rental agency, whom they called using the same helpful motorist's cell phone.

One of the friendly, patient police officers who had arrived at the scene offered to drive them back to their house, but when he caught a glimpse of Terri's face, ashen and still very much in shock, he said, "Hey, there's a diner just a little way down the road. How about we go grab a cup of coffee and then I'll take you back to Middletown? My shift's just about over and I don't mind the wait."

Jacques, realizing right away that the last place his wife wanted to go right now was in a car, replied, "That would be great, Officer Hardy. I think we could both use a little breather right now. Are you sure you don't mind?"

"No, of course not," Officer Hardy said. "You two have had quite a night! Just be glad nobody got hurt in all this, that's all."

Now, as the couple sat side by side at the counter in the diner, sipping their twin cups of coffee, both agreed that a bad meal, a disappointing show, and having had their car impounded were all rather trivial things to be upset about. What mattered most was that they had both escaped that evening with their lives. ■

1. **What is the setting of this story when it first begins?**
   A. an automobile pound
   B. New York City
   C. a diner
   D. a car rental agency

   HINT: This question asks you to think about the way the text is organized. Where do you think the author would mention the setting of the story?

2. **Why did Jacques and Terri rent a car?**
   A. They were unable to find a ride home.
   B. They had no money to pay for a parking ticket.
   C. The impound lot was closed until morning.
   D. The bus was scheduled to arrive much too late.

   HINT: Jacques and Terri decide to rent a car after receiving some information from a police officer. What was that information?

3. **How did the rental car catch on fire?**
   A. The manager of the rental car agency had put no oil in the car.
   B. Jacques and Terri drove the car until it ran out of gas.
   C. Jacques had accidentally ran the car into a large truck.
   D. The car had hit a mattress and dragged it along the road.

   HINT: This question asks you to recall a detail from the passage. If you are unsure of the answer, reread the middle of the passage.

4. **The purpose of the first three paragraphs is to**
   A. illustrate that something terrible had happened to Jacques and Terri.
   B. summarize the events that brought Jacques and Terri to the diner.
   C. foreshadow what will happen when Jacques and Terri leave the diner.
   D. describe why Jacques and Terri were traveling home from New York City.

   HINT: This question asks you to think about why the author wrote the first three paragraphs. Reread the paragraphs. What did you think the author was trying to say?

5. **Which of the following best describes how Jacques and Terri felt while at the diner?**
   A. surprised and happy
   B. calm and relieved
   C. angry and frightened
   D. cold and shaken

   HINT: Think about the way the characters were acting and talking at the diner. Which answer option best represents the way they felt?

6. **What would most likely have happened if Jacques had swerved around the mattress?**
   A. He and Terri would have taken the mattress home.
   B. He and Terri would have made it home safely.
   C. He and Terri would have gone to the diner to eat.
   D. He and Terri would have gone back to New York City.

   HINT: This question asks you to predict what might have happened in the story. If they had not hit the mattress, how do you think the story would be different?

7. **Why did Jacques agree to go to the diner even though it was so late?**
   A. He was afraid that the officer's patrol car would catch on fire.
   B. He knew his wife didn't want to get back in a car.
   C. He couldn't remember where they lived.
   D. He hadn't eaten any dinner that evening.

   HINT: This question asks you to recognize a detail from the story. Do you remember why the couple didn't head home right away?

8. **What lesson does "Accidents Happen" teach?**
   A. A true friend will be there for you in times of need.
   B. Treat others the way that you want to be treated.
   C. Some troubles make others seem less important.
   D. If you fail to succeed the first time, try again.

   HINT: This question asks you to think about the moral of the story. What do you think the author's implicit meaning in the story is?

9. **The tone of a story puts the reader in the midst of the action, letting him or her live through the experience.**
   - **In "Accidents Happen," what caused the happy, expectant tone of the story to change? Explain.**

   Use specific information from the story and any additional insight to support your response.

_____

_____

_____

_____

_____

_____

_____

_____

_____

_____

_____

_____

10. When Terri and Jacques discovered that the police had impounded their car because it was illegally parked, Terri reacted almost disdainfully.
    • Following the last episode described in this story, what are Terri's thoughts and feelings about police officers likely to be? Explain.
    Use specific information from the story and any additional insight to support your response.

YOU TRY IT

DIRECTIONS **INTRODUCTION**	Read this story/passage and answer the questions that follow. This passage tells the true story of the disappearance of the crew of a ship in 1872. What was written about this tragedy caused it to become one of the greatest mysteries in maritime history.

The *Mary Celeste* Mystery–The Real Story

Have you ever heard of a ship named the *Mary Celeste?* Most people today have never heard of it. However, at one time, this ship was part of one of the most often told stories of an unexplained mystery on the high seas. The captain, his family, and the entire crew of the *Mary Celeste* disappeared without a trace.

The reason this ship's disappearance became one of the biggest mysteries in marine history is because it was the subject of several sensational articles and books. Dr. Arthur

Conan Doyle, the author of the Sherlock Holmes series, wrote several short stories about a ship named the *Mary Celeste*. In these stories, he told his version of what had happened to the crew of the *Mary Celeste*. He said that the crew was forced to hurriedly abandon the ship, leaving behind a table completely set with food. Also noted were a bloody sword and blood-splattered cabins.

2

When the short stories first appeared, they turned what had been a minor puzzle into one of the most famous legends of the sea. Books about the *Mary Celeste* also appeared, two of which were said to have been written from the information in diaries of actual crew members of the *Mary Celeste.* Each gave a different explanation of what had happened to the crew. In one account, the crew mutinied[1] and then sharks attacked and killed most of them. In another telling, the crew fell into a time warp, or a change in space and time whereby people or objects of one period can be moved to another.

In the end, the actual facts of what happened became clouded and the mystery surrounding the *Mary Celeste* grew. Yet, what happened aboard the ship is very different from the fictionalized account, which was largely accepted as fact by the public.

The *Mary Celeste* was built in Nova Scotia in 1861 and was officially dedicated as the *Amazon* the day she was launched. From the beginning, she was an unlucky ship. Her captain died within two days of the ship's naming. Her first voyage almost ended in disaster when she collided with a fishing pier. On her next voyage, she caught fire after colliding with another ship. Then, on yet another voyage, she ran aground. Sailors, who are typically very superstitious, began to think of the *Amazon* as unlucky. It was hard to find men willing to sail on her. Eventually, following major repairs to the vessel, the ship was renamed the *Mary Celeste.*

On November 16th, 1872, the *Mary Celeste* set sail from Staten Island, New York. She was bound for Genoa, Italy, carrying casks of alcohol. On board were Captain Briggs, his wife, their two-year-old daughter, and seven crew members. About a month later, Captain David Reed Morehouse of the brig Del Gratia saw the *Mary Celeste* as she was nearing the Mediterranean Sea in the area of Spain. He saw that the other ship was

---

[1]**mutinied** *refused to obey the orders of a person in authority on-board the ship*

sailing erratically, as if it were out of control. But no distress flags flew from the masts.

After following the *Mary Celeste* for two hours, Morehouse came alongside and hailed the ship. There was no reply from those on board, so he sent a boarding party over to investigate the situation. The boarding party found the ship deserted. Everything seemed to be in order except that the crew were missing. The boarding party believed that the crew had left in a great hurry.

Some things were missing; the chronometer[2], the sextant[3], and the ship's papers were gone. However, the crew's gear and personal items were still stored in their normal places on the ship. The last entry in the log, which had been made ten days earlier, said that the *Mary Celeste* had just passed the Island of Santa Maria in the Azores of Portugal.

The boarding party also noticed other strange things. There was a lot of water between decks. Many items in the captain's quarters and where the crew slept were soaked. However, one pump was still functioning. The ship was not in danger of sinking. It looked as though the crew had launched the only lifeboat in an orderly fashion, rather than in a desperate attempt to flee the ship. The strange things Doyle had written about in his stories also were not found.

CHECK FOR UNDERSTANDING

Why do you think the disappearance of this ship became such a popular topic for stories?

All who had boarded the boat agreed that the crew had left the ship in an orderly fashion. There was no evidence of foul play. No one could say, though, why an experienced captain and his crew would leave a good ship. Yet, for some reason, the captain, his family, and the crew must have felt their ship was in some type of danger. They then abandoned it and were lost at sea.

The most believable and plausible theories about what happened to the *Mary Celeste* are based on the barrels of alcohol that the ship was supposed to carry from New York to Genoa, Italy. Captain Briggs had never hauled such dangerous cargo before. When the ship was unloaded, nine of the barrels were found to be empty. Nine leaking barrels would have caused a buildup of vapor in the hold[4]. Historian Conrad Byers believed that Briggs had ordered the hold to be opened, resulting in a immense rush of fumes

---

[2]**chronometer** *a timekeeping device*

[3]**sextant** *an instrument used to measure the altitude of an object above the horizon; used by navigators to calculate position on a nautical chart*

[4]**hold** *the lower, interior part of a ship where cargo is stored*

and then steam. Believing the ship was about to explode, Briggs had then ordered everyone into the lifeboat. However, perhaps because he was rushing, he may have failed to properly secure the lifeboat to the ship with a strong towline. The wind may have then picked up and blown the *Mary Celeste* away from her crew.

In 2005, German historian Eigel Wiese expanded upon Byers's ideas. He suggested that scientists at University College London create a reconstruction of the *Mary Celeste*'s hold to help them imagine and test what might have happened. Using butane as the fuel and paper cubes as the barrels, the smaller-size hold was sealed and the vapor was ignited. The force of the explosion blew the hold doors open and shook the scale model. However, none of the paper cubes were damaged, nor even left with scorch marks. Wiese's theory may explain why there was cargo still on the ship that looked to be undamaged. A break in the ship's rail might possibly have been caused by one of the hold doors bursting open.

If Wiese is correct, this burning in the hold would have been violent and perhaps enough to scare the crew into lowering the lifeboat. At the same time, the flames would not have been hot enough to have left burn marks. A frayed rope trailing in the water behind the ship might be evidence that the crew remained attached to the ship, hoping that the emergency would pass. The *Mary Celeste* was abandoned while its sails were at their fullest, and a storm was recorded to have happened not long afterward. It is possible that the rope to the lifeboat broke because the *Mary Celeste* was under full sail and therefore too strong for the little lifeboat.

No matter what really happened, people continue to be fascinated by the *Mary Celeste*'s disappearance, even if it isn't as well known today. Scientists continue to explore the possibilities of what might have happened to this unfortunate ship, her captain, and her crew. ■

1. **Why did the author most likely write this passage?**
   A. to explain how some mysteries continue for a long time
   B. to describe what it was like to work aboard a cargo ship
   C. to tell readers a story of great adventure on the high seas
   D. to show readers the jobs that a ship's crew had to do

   HINT: This question asks you to think about the author's purpose. Think about what you have read. What do think the author was trying to say?

2. **In paragraph 2, the word "version" means**
   A. diary.
   B. account.
   C. lesson.
   D. memory.

   HINT: This question asks you to identify the meaning of the word "version." Reread paragraph 2. Are there any clues to the word's meaning in the paragraph?

3. **What happened on the *Amazon's* first voyage?**
   A. The ship got stuck on the shore.
   B. The ship burst into flames.
   C. The ship hit a fishing pier.
   D. The ship ran into another ship.

   HINT: This question asks you to recall a detail from the passage. If you are unsure of the answer, reread paragraph 5.

4. **Where was the *Amazon* built?**
   A. New York
   B. Portugal
   C. Italy
   D. Nova Scotia

   HINT: This question asks you to recall a detail from the passage. Since the names of ships are in italics, it should be easy to recognize the first mention of this boat. Scan the passage looking for it.

5. Why was the *Amazon* probably renamed the *Mary Celeste*?
   A. because the ship was bought by another captain
   B. so sailors wouldn't think the ship was unlucky
   C. because *Amazon* wasn't a very pretty name
   D. so people would know where the ship came from

HINT: *This question asks you to make a judgment based on the passage. Knowing what you do about the Amazon, which answer choice best describes why they would have renamed the ship?*

6. Why did boarding party think the crew of the *Mary Celeste* had left in a hurry?
   A. Food was left sitting on the table.
   B. The ship's papers were missing.
   C. Personal items were left behind.
   D. They found a sword on the ship.

HINT: *This question asks you to make a judgment based on the passage. What actions of the crew would make the boarding party think that the original crewmembers had left in a hurry?*

7. Why did the boarding party find it strange that the ship was abandoned?
   A. The ship was sailing straight and steady.
   B. The ship was not in danger of sinking.
   C. The lifeboat was still attached to the ship.
   D. There were no items missing from the ship.

HINT: *This question asks you to think about information from the passage. Which of the answer choices best describes why the party thought that the abandoned ship was strange?*

8. The author believes that the story of the *Mary Celeste* became a legend because of
   A. the sensational books that were written.
   B. the diaries of the *Mary Celeste*'s crew.
   C. the report that Captain Morehouse made.
   D. the proof found aboard the *Mary Celeste*.

HINT: *This question asks you to think about information from the passage. What did the author mention that might explain why the story of the Mary Celeste became legend?*

9. Diaries of crew members of the *Mary Celeste* and studies by historians about how the crew met their fate present different accounts of what actually happened.
   • **How do the accounts agree? Explain.**
   • **How do they differ? Explain.**
   Use specific information from the article and any additional insight to support your response.

10. Today, in our world of ocean liners and instant communications, ships don't face the same dangers and perils that the *Mary Celeste* did.

    • So, why would anyone – including scholars and historians – be interested in finding out more about the *Mary Celeste*? Explain.

    Use specific information from the article and any additional insight to support your response.

YOU TRY IT

DIRECTIONS INTRODUCTION	Read this story/passage and answer the questions that follow. When people hear the word "pigeons," they often think of the city birds that roost on buildings and foul the sidewalks. That is one kind of pigeon, but there is another kind – the homing or racing pigeon.

A Long Way from Home

Mario is a dedicated breeder and racer of pigeons. Like other breeders, he hopes his birds will produce young that will combine speed and endurance. These kinds of birds will improve his chances of winning pigeon flying competitions.

Mario's pigeon loft is an extension off his garage. It is where the birds are housed and fed, each in its own cage. Built into the loft is a trap door. Through this door, the pigeons enter when they return from a flight.

Every day, Mario carefully examines each of his birds to check for any injuries or illnesses. On a shelf near their food, he has various bottles and cartons containing medicines and other things to ensure his birds' health. As Mario stops by each cage, he talks to the bird inside and calls it by name. The birds "coo," seeming to respond to his voice.

Training a homing pigeon takes time and patience. Today, Mario has asked his brother Vincent to take six birds out for a training run. Vincent – better known as Vinny – is driving to the New Jersey shore for the weekend. When he reaches a designated spot near Atlantic City, he will stop and release the birds from their cages.

"Remember," Mario tells him, "wait until you see them circle and head north before you drive off. Then, call me and tell me the time they left."

Mario knows the distance from the release point to the loft. As each pigeon enters the loft through the trap door, Mario will note the time. Knowing the distance and the time it takes the pigeons to enter the loft lets him calculate the birds' flying speeds.

6

Unfortunately, Vinny calls to tell Mario, "I had a problem with my van and it was much later than we planned before I released the birds. Then, a sudden summer storm rolled in from Pennsylvania. It may delay their return. I'm sorry, but I did my best."

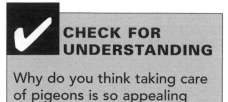

CHECK FOR UNDERSTANDING

Why do you think taking care of pigeons is so appealing to Mario?

Hanging up the phone, Mario begins the long, anxious wait for the pigeons to return. Early in the evening, the first bird enters through the trap door. A second and a third bird follow soon after. About half an hour later, a fourth and a fifth pigeon are safely home. One more to go!

An hour and a half later, the last of the pigeons has not returned. This worries Mario, and he gets up often during the night to see if the bird is back. However, each time he is disappointed. By the end of the week, Mario has to admit that the pigeon is lost. Something must have happened to it, probably caused by the storm, he thinks.

Three weeks later, as Mario goes through his mail, he finds a letter postmarked from Italy. The return address is from a man named Salvatore Genualdi in Genoa, Italy. Mario doesn't know anyone by that name. Why would this man be writing to him? He opens the envelope and reads:

Dear Señor Caruso,

Perhaps like you, I am a pigeon fancier. Last week, I found a strange, banded pigeon in my garden. After some coaxing, I managed to capture it—unharmed, of course. I knew its leg band would provide me with information about its owner. It took me a while to check on it, and I learned that the pigeon belonged to you: Mario Caruso in New Jersey.

I am sure that the pigeon did not fly all the way across the Atlantic Ocean from New Jersey to Italy. It most likely landed on a ship headed to the port of Genoa, probably blown off-course in a storm.

The pigeon is possibly one of your prize birds. I would be happy to get a cage and send it back to you. I could inquire to the cost. I am sure it will be quite expensive, and there is no guarantee that the bird will receive proper care on its return voyage. However, the decision is yours to make.

I will await hearing from you about what you wish me to do. In the meantime, your bird will be well cared for.

Sincerely, Salvatore Genualdi

Mario is astonished that his bird has wound up in Italy. He is grateful that another pigeon fancier had found it, however! He is even more appreciative that Senor Genualdi had traced the bird's owner and offered to arrange its return.

For a day, Mario considers his options and decides that it will be both costly and risky to try to have the bird returned. He sits down and writes a letter to Señor Genualdi.

DEAR SEÑOR GENUALDI,

I WAS BOTH SURPRISED AND DELIGHTED TO RECEIVE YOUR LETTER. YOU HAVE SOLVED THE MYSTERY OF WHAT HAPPENED TO MY LOST PIGEON.

THE DAY IT WAS RELEASED, THERE WAS A SUDDEN STORM. AS YOU SUGGEST, THE BIRD WAS PROBABLY BLOWN OFF-COURSE AND, FOR SURVIVAL, LANDED ON A PASSING SHIP.

I APPRECIATE YOUR GENEROUS OFFER TO ASSIST IN RETURNING THE BIRD TO ME. HOWEVER, I AGREE WITH YOU THAT DOING SO INVOLVES HIGH COST AND MUCH RISK, IN MY JUDGMENT, NOT WORTH TAKING.

PLEASE ACCEPT THE BIRD AS A GIFT FROM A VERY GRATEFUL AMERICAN PIGEON FLYER.

SINCERELY, MARIO CARUSO

Mario ponders the episode as he signs and seals his letter. At the same time, knowing the nature of pigeons, he isn't at all surprised at the bird's ingenuity. He can only hope that his little bird will enjoy his new life in Italy. And who knows? Maybe one day he will see it fly once more through his little trap door. ■

1. Why does Mario keep pigeons?

    A. to enter them in flying contests

    B. to protect them from bad storms

    C. to send messages to his friends

    D. to make sick birds well again

HINT: *This question asks you to recall a detail from the passage. If you are unsure of the answer, reread the first paragraph.*

2. Where does Mario keep his pigeons?

    A. in a garden

    B. at the shore

    C. in a loft

    D. on a ship

HINT: *This question asks you to recall a detail from the passage. If you are unsure of the answer, reread paragraph 2.*

3. What does the word "calculate" mean in the sixth paragraph?

    A. improve

    B. compare

    C. describe

    D. determine

HINT: *This question asks you to identify the meaning of the word "calculate." Reread paragraph 6. Are there any clues to the word's meaning in the paragraph?*

4. What was the first problem Vinny faced?

    A. There was a problem with the cages.

    B. A sudden storm rolled into the area.

    C. There was a problem with his van.

    D. One of the birds got stuck on a ship.

HINT: *This question asks you to think about information from the passage. If you are unsure of the answer, reread paragraph 6.*

5. When did Mario admit to himself that the last pigeons had been lost?

    A. after his brother called him

    B. at the end of the week

    C. over three weeks later

    D. when the fifth bird returned

HINT: *This question asks you to think about information from the passage. If you are unsure of the answer, read paragraph 9.*

6. How did Mario most likely feel when he got a letter from Italy?

   A. surprised

   B. annoyed

   C. disappointed

   D. embarrassed

HINT: Which of the answer choices best describes how you think Mario would have felt?

8. Why did Mario tell Señor Genualdi to keep the pigeon?

   A. He didn't want the pigeon to be hurt on the way back.

   B. He thought that the pigeon would be happier in Italy.

   C. He didn't want to cause problems for Señor Genualdi.

   D. He thought that Señor Genualdi needed a new pigeon.

HINT: This question asks you to think about information from the passage. Knowing what you do about Mario, why do you think he would tell Señor Genualdi to keep the pigeon?

7. Mario thinks that the reason the pigeon landed on a ship was because

   A. the pigeon had been badly hurt.

   B. the pigeon was trying to survive.

   C. someone had tried to steal the pigeon.

   D. a storm had blown the pigeon onto the ship.

HINT: This question asks you to recall a detail from the passage. If you are unsure of the answer, reread the letter that Mario wrote to Señor Genualdi.

9. Why did the author most likely write this passage?

   A. to describe to readers what pigeons are like

   B. to explain why some people race pigeons

   C. to show readers how to care for pigeons

   D. to tell a story about an astonishing event

HINT: This question asks you to identify the author's purpose. Think about what you have read. What do you think the author was trying to say?

10. Authors often include in their fictional stories events that could happen in real life.
    • Do you think that anything in this story could really happen? Explain.
    Use specific information from the story and any additional insight to support your response.

_____

_____

_____

_____

_____

_____

_____

_____

_____

_____

_____

_____

_____

11. When the structure of a story is chronological, events are told in the order in which they happen. Another structural feature of "A Long Way from Home" is the use of letters within the narrative.
    - How do the letters between Mario Caruso and Salvatore Genualdi affect the way the whole story is organized? Explain.

    Use specific information from the story and any additional insight to support your response.

CHAPTER 4

Expanding the Text
Predicting Meaning, Questioning, and Identifying Literary Conventions

RSL.6.10, RSI.6.10: QUESTIONING, CLARIFYING, PREDICTING
RSL.6.4, RSI.6.4 LS.6.5: LITERARY ELEMENTS/TEXTUAL CONVENTIONS

In this chapter you will work on two important comprehension skills: **predicting** and **questioning**.

Making predictions before, while, and after reading helps you understand the events in a story and draw conclusions about events in the future. Asking yourself questions about a text before, while, and after reading helps a reader check his or her understanding about what has happened so far in a story; confirm or create new predictions; and make personal connections to a text.

It is important to understand **literary elements and textual conventions** used in the text, and why a certain figure of speech is used to describe what a character in a story is saying or doing.

YOU TRY IT
You have just finished the first four chapters of a story, and there are several more chapters to go. Your teacher asks you to write a paragraph predicting what will happen next.
- Do you think about what has happened so far and what you know about the characters?
- Do you think about a time when you might have been in a similar situation to that of the characters in the story?
- Do you write down what you have imagined will happen in the story?

You should combine all these exercises, if you can. Then make the best prediction.

RSL.6.10, RSI.6.10: QUESTIONING, CLARIFYING, PREDICTING

PREDICTING OUTCOME

One of the ways to predict outcome is to relate what you are reading to your own life. You may think of an experience of your own or one that a friend has had that was similar to the situation in a story.

Predicting means expecting something to happen, telling what is going to happen, and being prepared for the outcome.

Sometimes you may read something that you really cannot relate to your own life. You may never have experienced the emotions or events that the characters are experiencing. Even in these cases, though, you can still think about the story and imagine what may happen.

LET'S TRY IT TOGETHER

> **DIRECTIONS**   Read these sentences from a famous story and we will discuss them.

Lion King

"Simba, everything you see exists together in a delicate balance," explains Mufasa. "As king, you will need to understand that balance and respect all creatures because we are all connected in the great circle of life." ■

Without knowing the context of the story, try to think about what the sentences are saying. Who do you think is speaking? Who is the speaker talking to? **Here are some questions you may ask in order to predict the meaning of the statement:**

• Can you think of a time when you might have told someone something like this?
• Have you ever had someone say something like this to you?
• What was the speaker feeling when he or she said this? What is the tone?
• If you had said this, what would you have been feeling?

LET'S TRY IT TOGETHER

DIRECTIONS   Read the story and together we will discuss the questions.

Laura and a Letter

A letter with foreign stamps was waiting on the hall table when Laura got home from school. After putting her books down and calling a greeting to her mom, she plopped down into the easy chair. She carefully opened the letter. It was from her pen pal, Megan, who lived in New Zealand. The girls were the same age and had been writing letters to each other for over a year now.

This exchange had started one day when Laura's teacher presented a unit on writing letters. He told the class about an organization that sets up contacts with young people in many countries who are interested in making foreign friends and corresponding with them by handwritten letter.

Laura liked to write and she thought she might enjoy having a pen pal. Now, whenever Megan's letters arrived, she couldn't wait to read what her friend had to say, and to respond.

Laura and Megan had written to each other about the weather, holidays, favorite things to do, family members and activities, and – of course – about school. While their daily lives have been different, they were surprised to learn just how much they had in common.

As Laura read the letter, her expression changed from one of quiet interest to that of animated excitement. Suddenly, she jumped up and, taking the letter with her, ran to find her mom. "Mom, you're not going to believe this! Guess what's in Megan's letter!" ■

1. **What will happen next in this story?**
   • What could Megan have written to make Laura so excited?
   • What exciting thing could she have read in the letter?
   • Will the letters continue or is something different about to happen?

2. **In one sentence, summarize how you would write the next part of this story.**

UNDERSTANDING THE TEXT

You likely know how important it is to really think about what you are reading rather than simply passing your eyes over the words. By thinking critically about what you are reading, you will both improve your understanding and, hopefully, increase your enjoyment.

A good way to think critically about a text is through questioning. **Questioning** means to ask yourself all sorts of things about a passage or story. For instance, you might ask yourself why a certain character does something mean to another character. What could have motivated that character to act the way he or she did? Is it possible that the character is jealous?

Here's another example of a question you could ask yourself about a text. Let's say that you are reading a passage about some friends having a barbecue at a park. You might ask yourself what materials and items the friends would need for a successful barbecue. Have you been to a barbecue? What things would you bring?

You also might ask yourself questions about the way a certain text is written. For instance, say an author goes into great detail in describing a particular building. You might ask yourself why that particular building is so important. Perhaps the building itself will play an important role in the story.

Here are some tips for asking good questions:

Think about why a character says, does, thinks, or feels things. If you can figure out the causes and motivations – the WHY's – for a character's behavior, you will gain a deeper understanding of the text.

Think about the details given and the details that are missing. Identifying important details in a text will help you to understand the WHO's, WHAT's, WHEN's, and HOW's. Figuring out which details are missing from a passage or story will indicate which questions need to be answered later in the text.

What is clarifying?

Sometimes what you read is complicated. When this happens, it is probably a good idea to stop while you're reading and ask yourself if you've understood what the passage is saying so far. Then go on and continue reading until you come to another place where you need to stop and think. Understanding what you read is important when you are trying to explain what you have read and to answer questions about the text.

Here are questions that you may be asked that would require you to make something clearer:

- What is the theme or central idea of the passage?
- How does the author think or feel about the topic?
- How did the writer approach the topic?
- Who is the audience the author was trying to reach?
- Compare and contrast by telling what or who is the same and what or who is different in the text.

LET'S TRY IT TOGETHER

> **DIRECTIONS**   Using your understanding of questioning, clarifying, and predicting, answer the open-ended questions following this text.

Peer Tutor

"I'd like to know more about the new peer-tutoring program," Sean said, walking down the hall at school with Miguel. "I think I'd like to help someone who's struggling. What do you think?"

"That does sound like a good program, especially for someone like me who has a hard time in Language Arts class," replied Miguel. "For me, though, I'm thinking about the Chess Club."

"It's so weird that we're such good friends – we have a ton of similar interests – and yet we're good at totally different things. I love Language Arts class! You always were good at chess, though, and I'm sure you'll enjoy the club," Sean replied, nodding in agreement. "Well, I think I'm going to stay late today and talk to Ms. Boyle about signing up. But I'm off to Math now – see you later!"

Later on that day, Sean went to find the faculty advisor, Ms. Boyle, who was in charge of the peer-tutoring program. As he entered the tiny office, he said, "Hello, Ms. Boyle. I was wondering if now would be a good time to find out about becoming a peer advisor."

Ms. Boyle smiled and gestured toward an empty seat across from her desk. "Sure, Sean. Have a seat. This is a new program that we developed because some students need one-on-one tutoring. Without help, they are going to have a very difficult time succeeding. While the teachers can identify these students' needs, we're willing to try a new idea in order to assist them: having these students work with other kids their own age."

"So, how do you match the students up with each other?" Sean asked.

"Well, we need to study your academic record and your other interests," Ms. Boyle explained. "Then we'll try to match you with students who are interested in some of the same things. That way, you two will have other things to talk about. If you want to, you can fill out this short form and we can get you started right away." ∎

1. What questions might have been on the form that Ms. Boyle asked Sean to fill out? Explain.

Here are questions to ask yourself before writing:
- What qualities would a good tutor need to have?
- What would an advisor need to know about a possible tutor?
- What would the advisor ask about the possible tutor's interests?
- Have you ever been tutored before, or known someone who has? What helped you or that person most in that situation?
- Is there a certain schedule that needs to be worked out ahead of time?
- What additional information might the advisor need to know to match up tutors with their students?

Write your answer on the lines below.

2. Based on what you know about the characters and the circumstances, predict what will happen next in this story.

How do I guess what is going to happen?

The fun thing about questions like this is that you can take the story in your own direction. However, you should map out what you are going to say before you write it. Think carefully about what you have read so that you can most accurately predict what might be likely to happen next.

Here are questions to ask yourself before writing:

- What do I know about the characters?
- Where did the passage leave off?
- Have I ever had a similar experience?
- Are there hints in the story about what will happen next?
- What will happen first, next, and last?

Write your answer on the lines provided.

How can I predict meaning?

You can predict meaning by anticipating what the author is going to say as the story goes on.

One of the ways to do this is to relate what you are reading to your own life. You may think of an experience of your own or one that a friend had that was similar to the situation in the story.

For example, if the story is describing moving to a new town, you may remember a time when your family moved. You may relate the characters in the story to people you actually know, both the good friends you left behind and the new friends you made. As you think about your own experiences, you may come up with an idea of what will happen next in the story based on what has happened to you.

Even if you have never had the experience that the characters in the story are having, you can still think about the story and imagine what may happen.

LET'S TRY IT TOGETHER

DIRECTIONS   Read the story/passage and together we will discuss the questions.

The Package

Oscar had been waiting for this box to arrive. Its contents could mean the difference between utter failure and outstanding success. Oscar examined the contents of the package. He could not believe his luck! This was just too much to accept. ■

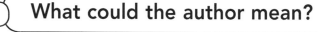

What could the author mean?

In the paragraph, the author states that the character Oscar "could not believe his luck," and that whatever was in the box was "just too much to accept." Based on this short paragraph, it seems that the author could mean two things by this. It could be that the author means that Oscar could not believe his GOOD luck. In that case it would seem that he felt the "outstanding success" was "too much to accept." In other words he was overwhelmed by this fortunate outcome.

However, the author could mean that Oscar could not believe his BAD luck. In that case it would seem that he was angered by the "utter failure" for which he felt himself destined.

RSL.6.4, RSI.6.4, LS.6.5: LITERARY ELEMENTS/TEXTUAL CONVENTIONS

What is a figure of speech?

One of the many ways that writers put life into their work is by using figures of speech. Figures of speech extend the range of what an author can tell us.

An author may use **figures of speech** to make her or his writing more appealing, more engaging, more exciting, and even more amusing.

Once you have learned how to work with and understand figures of speech, you can make your own writing livelier, more interesting, and more enjoyable to read and get more from what you read.

FIGURATIVE LANGUAGE

Figurative language, which uses figures of speech, is an imaginative and colorful way for an author to express him- or herself without coming right out and directly stating something.

Once you have learned how to work with figures of speech, you can make your own writing livelier, more interesting, and more enjoyable to read. You will also be able to better understand what you have read.

Among the many figures of speech, you may already be familiar with are **similes, metaphors, alliteration, personification, hyperbole, onomatopoeia,** and **idioms**.

SIMILE

A **simile** is a figure of speech where something is compared to something else, using the words *as* or *like*.

In a simile, two unlike things are explicitly compared. For example, someone in an uncomfortable situation might think, "I feel *like* a bug under a magnifying glass."

Examples: He's as busy *as* a beaver.
The snow is as thick *as* a blanket.

Try to write three similes of your own.

_____

_____

_____

METAPHOR

A **metaphor** is also a comparison. However, it does not use the words *as* or *like* in the way a simile does.

Another way to say this would be that a metaphor uses an expression or a word to refer to something it does not literally mean in order to suggest a similarity.

Examples: He was boiling mad.
Your comment gives me food for thought.

Try to write three metaphors of your own.

_____

_____

_____

ALLITERATION

The figure of speech called **alliteration** is described as using two or more words of a word group that begin with the same letter.

Spoken aloud, an alliterative phrase or sentence gives us an expressive way to hear the rhythm of language in the repetition of sounds. Alliteration is commonly used in poetry, jingles, advertisements, headlines, and tongue twisters.

Examples: **f**uss and **f**eathers
jump for **j**oy
Bertha **B**artholomew **b**lew **b**ig, **b**lue **b**ubbles.

Try to write three alliterative statements of your own.

_____

_____

_____

PERSONIFICATION

The figure of speech called **personification** gives human traits to other living things or to objects. In other words, it makes "persons" of them.

Human traits are the qualities, feelings, actions, and characteristics that people have. Other living things include plants and animals.

Examples: The playful waves hit the shore.
The smiling sun cast warmth on the park.

Try to write two sentences of your own that use personification.

_____

_____

HYPERBOLE

The figure of speech called **hyperbole** is the use of exaggeration to emphasize a feeling, an effort, or a reaction.

Hyperbole is the figure of speech where deliberate exaggeration is used for effect.

Examples: I'm so hungry I could eat a horse!
I've told you a million times not to exaggerate!

Try to write two sentences of your own that use hyperbole.

ONOMATOPOEIA

The figure of speech called **onomatopoeia** is the use of words that imitate the sound they describe.

In onomatopoeia, the sounds literally make the meaning. The word imitates a noise or an action.

Examples: Slurp!
Pow!
Buzz!
Oink

Try to write three examples of onomatopoeia.

IDIOM

An **idiom** is a way of speaking that is typical to a people or a place.

In this way, idioms are one of the hardest things for people studying a new language to understand because they cannot be guessed from the meanings of the individual words.

Examples: Drop me a line!
You're making a mountain out of a molehill.

While you may already know what the idioms above mean, here are some others:

Idiom	Meaning
drop someone a line	write to someone
Do you get it?	understand something
keep you're fingers crossed	hope for the best
make a mountain out of a molehill	make something seem much more important than it really is
over one's head	too difficult or complicated for someone to understand
fire someone	dismiss someone from a job because of poor performance

Try to write at least five idioms.

_____

_____

_____

_____

SPECIAL TYPE

Sometimes authors use special kinds of type in their writing. They do this for different reasons.

Examples of special type are *italics*, all **CAPITAL** letters, and **bold** lettering.

The main reason that authors use special type is for **emphasis**. The author wants the reader to pay special attention to a word in special type, to be able to understand why this word is important, and to know why the author is emphasizing it in this part of the passage.

Examples: Mom, can I go to the party, *please*?   (italics)
            Joey! Come back here, NOW!   (capital letters)

Another reason is to make the writing **clearer** and more precise. A person's thoughts may be in *italics*, while spoken words will be in quotation marks.

Example: Gabe and his family took a long trip to the family reunion. Gabe was looking forward to seeing his cousin Colin. He hadn't seen him in four years. When they arrived at the reunion, Gabe was so surprised to be greeted by a tall young man. "Hi, I'm Colin. Welcome to the reunion!" All Gabe could think was *I never would have recognized him. He looks so different!*

Bold lettering is used for emphasis because it catches the reader's eye. An author may use bold lettering to call your attention to certain words.

Examples: A **noun** is a person, place, or thing.
            The makeup test will be held this **Friday**, June 3.

You should look for different kinds of type throughout all of the passages you read. The special type may indicate that the author wants you to pay close attention to something.

YOU TRY IT

DIRECTIONS The following two editorials appeared in a magazine and a newspaper, respectively. Both authors of the editorials have strong opinions about the existence of "mythical" creatures.

Lake Monsters: Fact or Fiction?

1 Accounts of lake monsters exist on most continents. Regardless of where you live, recorded stories of resident monsters are common, especially in areas with large lakes. All reported lake monsters seem to have a number of things in common. They can only exist in large, deep, cold lakes. They are hard to see; in fact, only a few people claim to have ever seen them. Lake monsters are also camera-shy; the pictures that exist are blurry, so it is difficult to actually see the monsters being photographed. None has been known to attack or even to hurt anyone.

Sunday, January 8   **THE GLASSBORO GAZETTE**   **F5**

EDITORIAL
THERE ARE NO MONSTERS IN LAKES

Dear Editor:

I read your article in last month's "News You Need to Know" section ("Look Out for Lake Monsters!" June 2007) and I was appalled to see that the author truly believes that the stories of lake monsters are factual portrayals. It is high time that people recognize that lake monsters are about as real as flying unicorns! There is no scientific proof that they exist. In fact, much of the evidence to say that they are real has been shown to be false.

Scotland's Loch Ness Monster

✔ CHECK FOR UNDERSTANDING

What facts does each author use to support his or her opinion?

is probably the most famous of the lake monsters. However, one of the best photographs of the

so-called Loch Ness Monster was found to be a hoax in 1993. Colonel Robert Wilson did indeed claim to have photographed the creature in 1934. His photograph was the most convincing, certainly.

However, it was revealed that the object in the water was actually a plastic head mounted on the top of a toy submarine. Wilson did take the photograph, but what it shows is not the Loch Ness Monster.

Another proven hoax occurred in the area of Silver Lake in New York. In the 1800s, a local hotel owner created a "lake monster" and periodically put it in the lake to draw tourists – and tourism dollars – to the area. When the local hotel burned to the ground, firemen found the remains of a model of the reported Silver Lake Serpent in the ashes.

Today, the theory used to explain lake monsters is that they are

surviving prehistoric dinosaurs. The monsters are described as resembling something that looks like a plesiosaur, which is an aquatic reptile.

However, if you read local newspapers from a hundred years ago, you'll see that the descriptions of the lake monsters are different. In the 1800s, the monsters were described as long, snake-like beasts with mammal-like heads. Is it possible that the lake monster changed shape? I think not.

What is more probable is that people see what they have been told exists in the lake. They may be seeing something their imaginations make into a monster – a floating log with a branch sticking out of it, for example, obscured by dense fog.

see **No Monsters**, continued on page F6.

No Monsters,
continued from F5.

Another problem with proving the existence of lake monsters is that bones of large water animals have never been found in or around these lakes. One would assume that some of the monsters have died since they were first seen. Still, no monster-size bones have ever been found in or near lakes reported to have resident monsters.

There are many questions about these lake monsters. Dinosaurs have been extinct for millions of years; it is inconceivable that they still might exist today. Furthermore, a monster needs a lot of food and yet no lake with an alleged monster has ever reported a reduction in the fish population. How does the monster feed itself and its family?

It is time for people – including your reporter – to admit that lake monsters do not exist!

Sincerely,
Timothy Peters

Have Something to Say?

Submit an editorial to

THE GLASSBORO GAZETTE
Contact Pat Sullivan, Editor:
PSullivan@glassborogazette.com
or:
2304 East End Avenue
Glassboro, NJ 08028

EDITORIAL
MONSTERS DO EXIST, LIVE IN SOME LAKES

Dear Editor:

I'm so sick of people saying that lake monsters don't exist. I'm here to tell you that there are lake monsters! In North America, many deep lakes have stories about monsters told by the early American Indians.

Champ, the Lake Champlain monster, was seen by Samuel de Champlain when he sailed down the lake in 1609. Long before that, however, the Iroquois and the Abenaki mentioned such a creature and celebrated its existence. The Abenaki gave it the name Tatoskok. Tribal legends also tell of a monster in Canada's Lake Okanagan called Natiaka, meaning "the lake monster." There are many more examples, and many of these continue to be seen today. It is inconceivable that this many lake monsters could all be the work of pranksters. Too many have been seen for them not to exist.

Granted, there have been some famous hoaxes. Colonel Wilson's picture of the Loch Ness Monster, for example, was proven to have been fabricated. However, there are other pictures of the Loch Ness Monster that are not fakes. That monster does exist.

The study of animals whose existence has not yet been proven is known as cryptozoology. "Cryptids" often begin life as descriptions by people or as blurry photographs.

A number of these hidden animals have turned up alive and well over the years. Famous examples include the giant panda in 1869, the Komodo dragon in 1912, and the megamouth shark in 1976. Who is to say that this will not happen with some of the more famous lake monsters? Just because something has not been found does not mean that it doesn't exist. Many of these lake monsters are seen on a regular basis. Remember, it wasn't too long ago that some fishermen caught a so-called extinct fish!

I am sure that not all the lakes that purport to have a monster actually do have one. Many monsters have been created to boost tourism and make money, which is a very dishonest thing to do. However, there are some lakes where people have seen monsters for hundreds of years. Many of these lakes are connected to the ocean.

The truth is that the jury is still out. Scientists have not been able to prove or disprove the existence of lake monsters. Until we know for sure, just remember to take your camera along with you the next time you go to a large, deep lake. You just might be able to take a picture to show that a lake monster exists.

Cordially,
Joanna Mosley

---

1. The purpose of the first paragraph is to

A. explain how most lake monster reports can be disproved.

B. describe what most lake monster reports have in common.

C. show readers how many people made up fake lake monsters.

D. tell readers where the most lake monsters have been seen.

HINT: *This question asks you to think about why the author wrote a particular paragraph. Reread paragraph 1. What was the author's purpose?*

2. "Lake monsters are also camera-shy" means that

A. lake monsters swim too fast to be photographed.

B. lake monsters are too small to photograph.

C. few people are interested in lake monsters.

D. few pictures of lake monsters exist.

HINT: *This question asks you to predict what the author meant when he or she wrote a particular phrase. If you are unsure of the answer, reread the first paragraph.*

3. According to the author of "There Are No Monsters in Lakes," why did the hotel manager make a model lake monster?

A. to prove that the monster was real

B. to get people to stay at the hotel

C. to show how big the monster was

D. to keep people out of the lake

HINT: *This question asks you to think about information from the passage. If you are unsure of the answer, reread the fourth paragraph of the passage.*

4. According to the author of "There Are No Monsters in Lakes," what theory is used to explain lake monsters?

A. Lake monsters are actually dinosaurs.

B. Lake monsters are undiscovered species.

C. Lake monsters are actually large snakes.

D. Lake monsters can change their shapes.

HINT: *This question asks you to recall a detail from the passage. Skim the end of the article "There Are No Monsters in Lakes" to look for Timothy Peters's explanation.*

5. Which statement explains why the author of "There Are No Monsters in Lakes" thinks that so many people see lake monsters?

A. Many people are tricked by models of lake monsters.

B. Many people already believe that lake monsters exist.

C. Many people see things that they imagine are lake monsters.

D. Many people often mistake other animals for lake monsters.

HINT: *This question asks you to make a judgment about the passage. Read all of your answer options. Which best explains the author's opinion?*

6. The purpose of paragraph 13 is to

A. show readers that there is a history of lake monster sightings.

B. explain that new species have been discovered over the years.

C. describe the pictures of lake monsters that have not been faked.

D. tell readers that not all lake monster sightings can be proven.

HINT: *This question asks you to think about why the author wrote a particular paragraph. Reread paragraph 13. What was the author's purpose?*

7. In paragraph 16, the word "inconceivable" means

A. unacceptable.

B. uneventful.

C. unbelievable.

D. uninteresting.

HINT: *This question asks you to identify the meaning of the word "inconceivable." Reread paragraph 16. Are there any clues to the word's meaning in the paragraph?*

8. Both authors agree that

A. some people are too quick to believe in lake monsters.

B. some sightings of lake monsters have been hoaxes.

C. if lake monsters were real there would be bones.

D. there would be less fish if lake monsters were real.

HINT: *This question asks you to draw a conclusion based on the passage. Think about what you have read. Which of the answer options is something that both authors agreed about in the articles?*

9. "The truth is that the jury is still out" means that

   A. the truth about lake monsters will never be discovered.

   B. the truth about lake monsters will always interest people.

   C. no one understands where lake monsters came from.

   D. no one knows whether or not lake monsters really exist.

HINT: This question asks you to predict the meaning of a phrase used in the passage. This is an idiom, commonly used in American English. Have you heard someone say this before?

10. When he uses the phrase "lake monsters are about as real as flying unicorns," Timothy Peters means that

   A. lake monsters and flying unicorns can be found in the same areas.

   B. flying unicorns have been spotted for as long as lake monsters have been.

   C. flying unicorns are just as easy to find as lake monsters.

   D. lake monsters and flying unicorns are equally fake.

HINT: This question also asks you to identify the meaning of a phrase. Look at the way the phrase is worded. What do you think it means, since the author used the words "as real as"?

11. **People who see things that no one else even notices are sometimes said to have overactive imaginations.**

    • **Imagine that you have interviewed a lake monster enthusiast who is carrying out an investigation to determine once and for all whether or not monsters really do exist in one particular lake.**

    • **Write one of the questions you would like to ask this person and what you imagine would be the person's answer.**

    Use specific information from the article and any additional insight to support your response.

12. Joanna Mosley says, "Just because something has not been found does not mean that it doesn't exist."
    • **What does she mean by this statement? Explain.**
    Use specific information from the article and any additional insight to support your response.

YOU TRY IT

DIRECTIONS INTRODUCTION	Read this story/passage and answer the questions that follow. This passage tells about four women who proved that a woman is able to drive any type of car in any weather, particularly in the name of freedom.

Early Women Drivers Who Dared to Be Different

Alice Huyler Ramsey, photographed in 1910

In 1903, Dr. Horatio Jackson was the first person to drive an automobile from coast to coast. Most people thought that only men were capable of making this difficult journey, but four pioneering women challenged that concept. Their efforts gave women the same claim to the driver's seat as men had.

At that time, the road system in the United States was almost non-existent. There were streets and roads in and around cities and towns, but even there asphalt roads were a rarity. Most highways between towns were little more than wide cow paths. Car breakdowns and flat tires were common. There were no gas stations outside the towns, and driving a car was difficult and dangerous.

The idea of a woman driving from coast to coast was first proposed as a publicity stunt to sell cars. Carl Kelsey was the manager of the Maxwell-Briscoe Company, which made a car called the *Maxwell DA*. He asked Alice Huyler Ramsey to drive one of his cars across the country in 1909. Ramsey, who was the founder and president of the first Women's Motoring Club in the United States, agreed.

On June 6, 1909, Ramsey climbed into the driver's seat of her 30-horsepower *Maxwell DA*. She released the brake and started on a 3,800-mile cross-country

> ✔ **CHECK FOR UNDERSTANDING**
>
> Why do you think it was so unusual to have a woman drive cross-country? Why would it spark public interest?

trip from New York City to San Francisco. Although three women accompanied her, Ramsey was the only one who knew how to drive. Most people predicted that she would return home in a matter of days.

The trip took 59 days. Ramsey herself did all the driving and the repair work, such as changing spark plugs and fixing flats. The trip was not without incidents, however. In Nebraska, for instance, a sheriff's posse looking for two murderers halted them. At times, when Ramsey got lost, she would drive to high ground and look for telegraph poles. Then, they would follow the telegraph poles into the next town.

Later on, in Utah, the bolts holding the front wheels together broke when the car hit a prairie-dog hole. A blacksmith had to put the car back together. Also in Utah, they ran into so much mud that it took them 13 days to cross the state. Daily mileages ranged from four to 198 miles. In all, Ramsey wore out 11 sets of fabric tires in her drive cross-country. Figure 1 shows Ramsey's route. Ramsey drove across the United States 70 more times. She did it once a year until her death at the age of 96.

Blanche Stuart "Betty" Scott drove across the United States in 1910. In an effort to publicize their automobiles, the Willys-Overland Company sponsored Betty and a female reporter named Gertrude Buffington Phillips. The car was the Lady Overland. The pair drove from New York City to San Francisco.

While passing through Dayton, Ohio, Scott saw a Wright plane flying overhead. She knew immediately that she wanted to learn to fly. Scott subsequently became the first female to fly solo in an airplane. In fact, the publicity surrounding Scott's automobile journey was what attracted the attention of Jerome Fanciulli and Glenn Curtiss, who agreed to provide her with flying lessons in Hammondsport, New York. Today, Betty Scott is known more for her barnstorming antics than for being the second woman to drive cross-country in an automobile.

In early 1915, another group of women drove across the United States. This time, however, they were not looking to publicize the automobile; they wanted to champion the cause of giving women the right to vote in public elections. Sara Bard Field, a poet, wanted to bring signatures supporting women's right to vote to President Woodrow Wilson in Washington, D.C. Two women in San Francisco agreed to drive her to the nation's capital.

The only cross-country road at that time was called the Lincoln Highway. However, it was not much better than a wagon trail. There were few maps, no gas stations along the highway, and no motels. At each major city, Field spoke to large crowds and obtained more signatures supporting women's right to vote.

This trip was also not without its problems. In Wyoming, the women had to push their car through snowdrifts. In Kansas, their car had to be towed out of several mud holes.

When Field reached Washington, she gave the petitions to President Wilson. He remarked that he had never seen so many signatures in one place before. Following the ride, Field returned to California and continued writing poetry.

Later, in 1915, Anita King, a racecar driver-turned-actress, drove solo cross-country. All she had for company was her large English bulldog. Like the others, she met many obstacles. One night, King was forced to kill a coyote that had attacked her. Another time, she almost had to shoot a dangerous wanderer who tried to rob her on a lonely stretch of road. After she had completed her trip, she returned to movie making.

Summary

One of the by-products of these pioneering women was that more people began to accept female drivers in all types of cars. These women had shown the world that they could survive in wilderness areas. They also proved that women were very capable of driving anywhere and in all types of weather. The publicity that surrounded their trips was also one of the factors that caused better roads to be built across America. ∎

1. What prefix can you add to "common" to make it mean "not common"?

    A. pre-

    B. non-

    C. un-

    D. re-

HINT: This question asks you to identify the prefix that could make the word "common" mean "not common." If you are unsure of the answer, try each of the answer choices out by saying them with the word "common."

2. Why was the idea of a woman driving across the country "first" proposed?

    A. to see if a woman could drive faster than a man

    B. to get people to buy a certain company's cars

    C. to map the fastest route across the country

    D. to help women receive the right to vote

HINT: This question asks you to recall a detail from the story. If you are unsure of the answer, reread the third paragraph.

3. Why did Carl Kelsey want Alice Huyler Ramsey to drive across the country?

    A. She was a very famous movie actress.

    B. She was a well-known racecar driver.

    C. She was the manager of a company that made cars.

    D. She was president of the first women's motor club.

HINT: This question asks you to think about information from the passage. If you are unsure of the answer, skim the beginning of the passage looking for hints.

4. Why did "most" people think that Alice Huyler Ramsey would return home after a few days?

    A. They didn't think that the trip across the country would take very long.

    B. They didn't think that a woman would be able to drive across the country.

    C. They thought that she would become lost without any road signs.

    D. They thought that she would become tired from making all the repairs.

HINT: This question asks you to draw a conclusion based on the information in the passage. At what time in history does the passage take place? How might that affect how people thought?

5. In which of the following states did Alice Huyler Ramsey face the "most" problems?
   A. Utah
   B. Nebraska
   C. Ohio
   D. New York

HINT: This question asks you to think about information from the passage. If you are unsure of the answer, reread paragraphs 5 and 6.

6. The author included "Figure 1" in the passage to
   A. describe why a national highway system was needed.
   B. tell readers why Alice Huyler Ramsey learned to drive.
   C. explain just how dangerous the drive across the country was.
   D. show readers the distance Alice Huyler Ramsey traveled.

HINT: This question asks you why the author included the map within the passage. Look back at Figure 1. Did it help you to understand the passage? How?

7. Why did the author put the word "Maxwell" in *italics***?**
   A. to emphasize its importance
   B. to indicate that it is being defined
   C. to show that it is the name of something
   D. to tell about its size

HINT: This question asks you to think about why the author wrote something a specific way. Think about what you know about the Maxwell. Why do you think the author put it in italics?

8. Why did Sarah Bard Field want to travel to Washington, D.C.?
   A. She wanted to encourage women to drive across the country all by themselves.
   B. She wanted to give the president signatures in support of a national highway system.
   C. She wanted to give the president signatures in support of women's right to vote.
   D. She wanted to write a book of poetry about her experiences while driving across the country.

HINT: This question asks you to recall a detail from the passage. If you are unsure of the answer, reread paragraph 10.

9. What made Alice King different from the other women drivers?

A. She had once been a well-known poet.

B. She had once been a racecar driver.

C. She took less time than the other drivers.

D. She had more help than the other drivers.

HINT: This question asks you to make a judgment based on the passage. Think back to the women mentioned in the passage. What made Alice King different?

10. What did Anita King do *after* she drove across the country?

A. She returned to making movies.

B. She returned to writing poetry.

C. She drove across country many more times during her life.

D. She drove to Washington, D.C. to meet with the president.

HINT: This question asks you to think about the information from the passage. If you are unsure of the answer, reread the end of the passage.

11. After Alice Huyler Ramsey agreed to drive a *Maxwell* from coast to coast, she set out in June 1909 with three passengers. The author writes, "Most people predicted that she would return home in a matter of days."
    • What do you think would have happened if it had turned out that the naysayers were right and Ramsey's trip had only lasted a few days? Explain.
    Use specific information from the article and any additional insight to support your response.

12. In the early twentieth century in the United States, women's roles in society were fairly set, but in some ways, they were open to change.
    • Imagine yourself as a young American woman in 1916.
    • Which opportunities would the ability to drive have opened up to you? Explain.
    Use specific information from the article and any additional insight to support your response.

YOU TRY IT

DIRECTIONS INTRODUCTION	Read this story/passage and answer the questions that follow. Sharks tend to have a pretty bad reputation because whenever they attract media attention, it's usually because of some unfortunate accident. Perhaps if people knew more about these animals, they would think better of them.

Little-Known Facts About Sharks

Sharks are among the most feared predators in the ocean. The sight of a big fin slicing through the water will spread fear up and down a beach in seconds. Yet, most people know very little about these notorious beasts.

1

In the newspapers, a lot of attention is paid to shark attacks when they occur. However, the number of people killed each year by sharks is actually less than the number of people killed by lightning, bees, or crocodiles. Sharks cause fewer than seven deaths a year.

2

Sharks have been on Earth since long before the dinosaurs. They have lived in the waters of this planet for over 400 million years. Like crocodiles, they have continued to evolve. Today, sharks are among the most efficient predators in the ocean.

There are about 400 species of shark alive today. About 80 percent of them never attack humans and are smaller than five feet in length. Of the remaining species, only six are considered dangerous to humans: the great white, the oceanic whitetip, the lemon, the tiger, the bull, and the hammerhead. Of these, the bull shark – the most dangerous – is credited with attacking humans the most.

Sharks are found in both salt water and fresh water. While most can only live in salt water, a few can live in both kinds of water. The bull shark is one such shark. There are

others. These include the square nose, slipway gray, and the river whaler. Lake Nicaragua in Nicaragua, seems to be a place that is known for having freshwater sharks.

Experts believe that most shark attacks occur because the shark can't recognize a swimmer among fish where it is feeding. Attacks will also occur when a shark believes it is scaring off an intruder, when it is mistakenly bumped into, or when it is accidentally stepped on. Unfortunately, even if a human has been bitten by mistake, he or she is usually in serious trouble.

Sharks attack in one of three ways:
- the hit and run,
- the bump and bite, and
- the sneak attack.

✔ **CHECK FOR UNDERSTANDING**

If most people know very little about sharks, then why do you think they are among the most feared creatures in the ocean?

The **hit and run** usually occurs in shallow waters. This type of attack is really a case of mistaken identity because the shark thinks that the swimmer is food. It may just be responding to being bumped or stepped on. Only after biting does the shark realize its mistake; it typically will then leave the area fairly quickly.

The **bump and bite** is more serious. Here, the shark has assessed the situation and has decided that it wants to attack. In this type of attack, the shark generally swims circles around its prey first, and then approaches and bumps the swimmer. After going around again, the shark then attacks. Serious injuries result from attacks of this kind.

The third type of attack, the **sneak attack**, results in the most serious injuries. The shark has decided to intentionally pursue the swimmer, treating a person as its prey. The shark will wait in ambush and then strike swiftly, taking multiple bites as it makes its pass. The shark returns again and again in this same fashion. Few swimmers live through this type of attack, but it is also very rare.

One misconception about sharks is that they have poor eyesight. Actually, just the opposite is true. The eye of a shark is seven times as powerful as a human cornea; in fact, shark eyes have even been used as a transplant for human corneas. A shark's eyes can also distinguish colors.

While it may be hard to believe, sharks can also be trained. Sharks have learned routines at the same rate as pigeons or white rats. There are also some species of sharks that do not need to move continually to survive.

There are even some sharks on the endangered list. The Australians have placed the great white and gray nurse sharks on the endangered list, making it illegal to hunt these sharks. Experts in other countries are also considering placing several other species of shark on the endangered list. ■

1. What does the word "notorious" mean in paragraph 1?

A. famous for bad reasons

B. capable of swimming

C. large or overweight

D. humorous or comedic

HINT: This question asks you to identify the meaning of the word "notorious." Reread paragraph 1. Are there any clues to the word's meaning in the paragraph?

2. What is the effect of comparing sharks to lightning, bees, and crocodiles in the second paragraph?

A. It shows that sharks are often most active during very bad thunderstorms.

B. It shows that sharks can be as scary and dangerous as crocodiles are.

C. It shows that sharks are not as dangerous as they sound in newspapers.

D. It shows that newspaper reporters do a poor job of writing about bee stings.

HINT: This question asks you to think about why the author compared two things. If you are unsure of the answer, reread paragraph 2.

3. Which sentence tells what this passage is mostly about?

A. Sharks use three main methods to attack people.

B. There is much about sharks that people do not know.

C. There are many different species of shark in the oceans.

D. Sharks live and hunt in salt water and fresh water.

HINT: This question asks you to identify the central idea of the passage. Think about what you have read. What do you think the author was trying to say?

4. According to the passage, how are sharks like crocodiles?

A. They are not on endangered species lists.

B. They are efficient ocean predators.

C. They swim in salt water and fresh water.

D. They evolved over millions of years.

HINT: This question asks you to draw a conclusion based on the passage. Where did the author compare sharks and crocodiles? If you are unsure of the answer, eliminate obvious wrong answer choices first.

5. **Why does a shark most likely take more than one bite when it decides to attack a swimmer?**
   A. to warn people to swim away
   B. to learn more about how the person tastes
   C. to make it difficult for the person to escape
   D. to scare whatever is under attack

   HINT: *This question asks you to make a conclusion based on the passage. Look at your answer options. Which is most likely the reason why sharks take more than one bite when they attack?*

6. **Which type of attack causes the *most* serious injuries?**
   A. the hit and run
   B. the bump and bite
   C. the sneak attack
   D. the bite and spit

   HINT: *This question asks you to recall a detail from the passage. If you are unsure of the answer, reread the section of the passage that talks about the types of shark attacks.*

7. **Which kind of shark can live in fresh water?**
   A. the oceanic whitetip shark
   B. the hammerhead shark
   C. the tiger shark
   D. the river whaler

   HINT: *This question asks you to recall a detail from the passage. If you are unsure of the answer, reread the middle of the passage.*

8. In "Little-Known Facts About Sharks," the author used special type and other organizational elements to help him describe three kinds of shark attacks.
• Why did the author organize the information in this way? Explain.
Use specific information from the article and any additional insight to support your response.

9. According to the author, most sharks are harmless to humans and they need our protection.
   - Do you think it is important to make sure that sharks don't disappear from the world's oceans? Explain.

   Use specific information from the article and any additional insight to support your response.

YOU TRY IT

DIRECTIONS
INTRODUCTION
Read this story/passage and answer the questions that follow. The following editorials appeared in a newspaper in 2002. Each has a different view about the issue of shark attacks on humans.

Balanced Discussion: Sharks

Sunday, January 8   **THE GLASSBORO GAZETTE**   **F5**

PERSPECTIVES
SHARKS NEED OUR PROTECTION

By Jaydon Schmidt

Jaydon Schmidt
Columnist

Some species of sharks are in danger of becoming extinct. We need to start protecting them or they will soon go the way of the dinosaurs.

Sharks are the media's common target. From what is reported in the newspapers each summer, one would think that the number of shark attacks on humans increases each year. Yet, this perception is totally false.

3 The number of shark attacks is either decreasing or has remained about the same for several years. In 2001, 55 people reported being attacked by sharks in the United States; that figure is one less than the attacks during the previous year. Around the world, only 76 unprovoked shark attacks happened in that same year, also less than the year before. Even the number of deaths worldwide due to shark attacks is down from 12 in 2000 to five in 2001.

The real danger is to the sharks. As many as 100 million are caught or killed each year. Many times, sharks are taken by accident when they get caught in fishing nets. Because of this, they are vulnerable to being over-fished and threatened as a species. In fact, fishing has reduced some species of shark almost to the level

"The real shark problem is attacks by humans on sharks."

of extinction. Sharks take a long time to mature and reproduce. If something is not done very soon, some species of shark will soon cease to exist.

5 Because its not reported that shark attacks are actually very rare, many people want sharks eliminated. They point to the one or two very serious attacks that occur each year. In fact, only three people died from shark attacks in the United States last year.

What we need is careful monitoring and control of people swimming in the ocean.

Sharks were on this earth before the dinosaurs. The ocean is their habitat. When we swim, we are using the water that sharks have been using for millions of years.

It is time we begin to realize that the real shark problem is attacks by humans on sharks. Little by little, we are exterminating the entire shark population. What we need are more realistic procedures for ensuring that both people and sharks can co-exist in the ocean. For example, sharks like to feed from dusk to dawn.

Humans should try not to go swimming during those times. We also know that bright, shiny objects attract sharks. Swimmers should never wear jewelry or bright objects while in the water.

These are just two of the things people can do to reduce the possibility of shark attacks. There

Balanced Discussion

are others. Lifeguards at beaches where sharks are known to swim need to enforce all the rules to protect humans. In this way, we can still allow people to swim in the ocean and save all species of shark for future generations.

✔ CHECK FOR UNDERSTANDING

What might have happened in Glassboro when this was written?

Sunday, January 8   THE GLASSBORO GAZETTE   F6

PERSPECTIVES
SHARKS AND PEOPLE MUST BE SEPARATED

By Ed Romburger

Ed Romburger
Columnist

Co-exist with sharks? Now I have heard everything! Imagine swimming in the same area as a predator that can take your leg off with one bite!

Last summer in three feet of water, an eight-year-old boy had his arm ripped off by a bull shark He survived only because of a dramatic rescue by his uncle. In Australia, sharks killed two surfers in just over 24 hours. Witnesses to one of the attacks said that a 15-foot shark struck the surfer not once but twice.

In the United States alone, there were 55 attacks by sharks on humans in one year. Each summer, newspapers report on the carnage caused by unprovoked shark attacks. It is time we did something to protect the people swimming in the ocean.

Some people would have sharks and humans co-exist in the same areas. They say that the sharks have more to fear from people than people have to fear from sharks. Tell that to the roughly 100 people who are attacked by a shark each year. Tell that to the people who have lost legs or whose wounds have required 300 stitches.

Isn't it time that we took steps to ensure that sharks do not swim in areas where humans swim? The truth is that nobody really knows why a shark attacks a person. Sharks are very unpredictable. The same shark will swim right by one swimmer and then attack another in the same area. People have been attacked in deep water,

"The truth is that nobody really knows why a shark attacks a person. Sharks are very unpredictable."

and some have also been attacked in less than three feet of water. Being both unpredictable and dangerous is a lethal combination.

We need to stop sharks from swimming in the areas where people go into the ocean. This can be done with the use of underwater fences around those swimming areas known to be frequented by sharks. Moreover, we should hire fishermen to hunt

sharks that are found near these areas of the ocean. Hunting for sharks will reduce the overall shark population.

When hunting is combined with the use of underwater fences, it will help to ensure the safety of bathers on those beaches where most shark attacks occur. Yes, this will add some expense initially; however, it will also save the lives and limbs of those people who venture out into the ocean. We can't stop people from swimming, but we can control sharks' access into the areas where most people swim.

1. **"Sharks are the media's common target" means that sharks**
   A. are often harmed by people accidentally.
   B. are reported negatively about quite frequently.
   C. are more dangerous than people think.
   D. are attacked and caught during fishing season.

HINTS: *This question asks you to predict what the author meant when he wrote a particular phrase. Skim-read the beginning of the first article. What do you think the phrase means?*

2. **Ed Romburger's article is mostly about**
   A. the best material to use for an underwater fence near beaches.
   B. the cost of putting people in the hospital after shark attacks.
   C. the reasons to keep sharks away from swimming people.
   D. the dangers of hunting sharks with too many fishermen.

HINT: *This question asks you to identify the central idea of one of the articles. Think about what you have read. What do you think Ed Romburger was trying to say?*

3. **Why does Jaydon Schmidt want to help save sharks?**
   A. He wants to protect them for the future.
   B. He believes that they can stop fish overpopulation.
   C. He thinks that sharks should be able to do anything.
   D. He feels that sharks are unfairly blamed for hurting people.

HINT: *This question asks you to think about Jaydon's point of view. What was his argument about why we should protect the sharks? If you are unsure of the answer, skim the first article for clues.*

4. **What is the purpose of paragraph 12?**
   A. to warn the reader not to swim around Australia
   B. to tell about the dangers of using a poor surfboard
   C. to describe the result of a set of shark attacks
   D. to show what happened in each of 55 attacks

HINT: *This question asks you to identify why the author wrote a particular paragraph. Reread paragraph 12. What do you think the author was trying to say?*

5. What does the word "eliminated" mean in paragraph 5?

A. chased

B. adopted

C. destroyed

D. scared

HINT: This question asks you to identify the meaning of the word "eliminated." Reread paragraph 5. Are there any clues to the word's meaning in the paragraph?

7. What is the purpose of paragraph 3?

A. to explain how the number of attacks has recently changed

B. to warn the reader that some attacks cannot be stopped

C. to tell the reader that lots of shark attacks are deadly

D. to show that sharks are not as dangerous as they seem

HINT: This question asks you to identify why the author wrote a particular paragraph. Reread paragraph 3. What do you think the author was trying to say?

6. Why does Ed Romburger believe we should separate sharks and people?

A. Humans have not lived as long as sharks have.

B. Sometimes shark attacks are unpredictable.

C. Sharks could find a way to chew through a fence.

D. There is no way to stop people from swimming.

HINT: This question asks you to recall a detail from the passage. If you are unsure of the answer, reread the middle of Ed Romburger's article. What is his opinion of sharks?

8. Why does a shark's slow reproduction process make it vulnerable?

A. It means sharks will not be over-fished by fishermen.

B. It makes it easier for sharks to be caught in fishing nets.

C. It is difficult for sharks to quickly replace those that have been killed.

D. It is common for sharks to live in shallow waters near beaches.

HINT: This question asks you to make a judgment based on the information in the first article. If you are unsure of the answer, reread the fourth paragraph.

9. Jaydon Schmidt supports measures that would establish a peaceful coexistence between sharks and human swimmers.
   • **Do you agree or disagree with Schmidt's position? Explain.**
   Use specific information from the article and any additional insight to support your response.

10. **"Sharks and People Must Be Separated"** is the view of Ed Romburger. His editorial concentrates on what happens when sharks and humans collide in the water.
    • **Is it possible to agree with what this writer has to say and, at the same time, to appreciate the positive contributions that sharks make to the balance of life in the ocean? Explain.**
    Use specific information from the article and any additional insight to support your response.

CHAPTER 5

Going Beyond the Text
Forming of Opinions; Making Judgments and Drawing Conclusions

RSI.6.8: MAKING JUDGMENTS/DRAWING CONCLUSIONS

To answer some open-ended questions, you will be asked to **form opinions** about what you have read. This chapter will review how to form a good opinion, first by gathering facts from the text, by analyzing how the author used the facts, and then by making an informed decision about how you will choose to express your thoughts.

Similarly, in some questions, you may be asked to **make a judgment** or **draw a conclusion**. While these two tasks may at first sound like they would be the same, there are differences in the way you would approach each. Before you answer the questions being asked, it is important to think about your point of view and plan what you want to say.

YOU TRY IT

You have just finished reading a story. Your teacher asks you to write your opinion of the actions of one of the characters in the story. What do you do?

- Do you describe the character's appearance and personality and tell facts about him or her?
- Do you tell all the things the character did in the story?
- Do you write down your feelings about the character?

Your best bet would be to do the last option. You should write what you thought about who the character was and what the character did.

FACTS AND OPINIONS

How often have you heard or asked this question: "What do you think?"
The response to this question would be your opinion.

An **opinion** is what a person thinks. Opinions can't be proven.

An opinion has no right or wrong answer. Whether or not you should take an opinion to heart depends on the honesty, integrity, and knowledge of the person who is speaking or the author who is writing.

A **fact** is based on real information and can be proved to be true.

A fact that is verified does not change from person to person or from place to place. It is simply an accepted fact. If you want to verify a fact, places to look include encyclopedias, dictionaries, an almanac, an atlas, and textbooks.

Here are some facts.
- The National Aquarium is located in Baltimore, Maryland.
- In 1893, two sisters from Louisville, Kentucky, composed the song "Happy Birthday to You."
- Street names for the game of Monopoly came from locations in or near Atlantic City, New Jersey.
- The first capital of the United States was New York City.

Here are some opinions.
- Being nice is better than being grouchy.
- This is the best birthday cake I have ever eaten!
- Sightseeing trips are the most enjoyable kinds of vacations.
- My little sister's preschool recital was just the cutest show!

When you read and listen to people, it is important for you to be able to tell the difference between facts and opinions.

NOW IT'S YOUR TURN!

To determine if a particular statement is a fact or an opinion, ask yourself – can I find out if this statement is true? If the answer is "yes", the statement is a fact. If the answer is "no", the statement is an opinion.

Read the sentences below. Determine which are facts and which are opinions. Circle the correct answer.

1   **My father is an excellent businessman.**
    FACT   OPINION

2   **There are four state capitals named after former U.S. presidents.**
    FACT   OPINION

3   **My sister placed fifth in the Youth Rally Marathon last month.**
    FACT   OPINION

4   **The last day of school is going to be a blast because we're having a picnic.**
    FACT   OPINION

ANSWERING OPEN-ENDED QUESTIONS

You may be asked to form an opinion about a passage and support your answer with facts and information from the text.

How would I write an answer to this kind of question?
You will have to think about the ideas and information in the article or story and then use them to back up your opinion. As you write your response, remember to connect your opinion to the story or article you have just read! That will make your argument or opinion much stronger.

For answering open-ended questions, remember to:
• Focus your response on the question asked.
• Answer all parts of the question.
• Give a complete explanation.
• Use specific information from the passage.

LET'S TRY IT TOGETHER

DIRECTIONS   Read the story and together we will discuss the questions.

Letter to the School Board

Dear School Board Members:

I am a sixth-grade student at Atlantic Middle School. I am writing to you about the proposal you are considering that would require a writing or math skills class for all middle-school students in our district, beginning next school year. Since there has recently been a lot of publicity about the proposal, our class has been reading the articles and discussing them. I would like to add my voice to the voices of all the parents, teachers, and students who do not want to see this proposal become a requirement for all students.

I think that requiring an extra course is not a good idea. I do understand that writing and math skills are important subjects. We get plenty of practice in our language arts and math classes. However, few students would be able to add another class to their schedules while continuing to get passing grades. In addition, I don't think that all of us have the time to take full advantage of an extra course. Personally I know that I don't.

I already feel that I spend too much time either being at school or doing homework. I would really like to have more time to do some things for fun. I would also like to have some time to spend with my family when I am not doing work for school.

I thought you might want to hear one student's opinion before making a final decision on this matter. Thank you for your time.

Sincerely, Lena Melo

---

1. How does Lena support her opinion?
Lena used facts to support her opinion. She decided what her opinion was on the topic, and then used information to help support her opinion.

- Most middle school students already have more than enough work to do.
- Few students would be able to add another class while continuing to get passing grades.
- Lena herself said she is already doing so much that she has no free time.

RSI.6.8: MAKING JUDGMENTS/DRAWING CONCLUSIONS

MAKING JUDGMENTS

Every day, people make judgments. You have probably made quite a few today already!

When you **make a judgment** about something you've read in a passage, you use what you already know together with information from the passage itself to make a decision.

Making a judgment can be effective in understanding what you are reading. While you are thinking about what you are reading, you are probably making judgments. You may be making a judgment about one of the characters, based on his or her actions in the story. You could also be making a judgment about the way characters interact with each other.

You have learned that sometimes authors do not come right out and say what they really mean. When that happens, the author is relying on the reader to make his or her own judgment about a character or about what will happen in a story.

Here are questions to ask yourself when making a judgment based on a passage:
• What is important? Why?
• How does the author lead the reader from one event to another?
• How does each event within the story affect the rest of the story?
• What do I know to be true from my own life?

Sometimes, an author may lead you to believe a character will act one way and then surprise you in the end by having the character end up doing something entirely different. When doing this, the author is assuming that you will be making a judgment while you are reading.

Authors tell readers much more than they come right out and say. They give you hints or clues to help you "read between the lines."

LET'S TRY IT TOGETHER

DIRECTIONS   Read the story and together we will discuss the questions.

Time Crunch

Caroline walked home from the school bus stop on Monday with a frown on her face. She was faced with a difficult decision. On Saturday, three events would be held, all at approximately the same time. She wanted to go to all three but that, of course, would be impossible. But each would be fun and rewarding for different reasons.

The annual bazaar and raffle were taking place at her school all day, but the things she really wanted to see and do all happened in the afternoon. The drawing of the winning raffle tickets was scheduled for 2:00 p.m. Immediately following that would be a performance by a visiting clown troupe. Caroline's teacher had told the class how entertaining the clowns' act was. Caroline and some of her friends had been looking forward to sitting together and laughing at the clowns, and they were all hoping to win the raffle prize.

A music concert would be held at the high school at various times throughout weekend. Her older brother Josh would be playing a solo trumpet piece around 2:00 p.m. on Saturday as well. After hearing him practice at home for many months, Caroline had really been looking forward to seeing him actually perform. Her parents and younger sister would be there, too, and her grandparents were hoping to come.

Caroline's best friend Erica, who lived next door, would be playing in a 2:00 game at the regional soccer tournament. Caroline herself played some soccer, but she didn't think she'd ever be able to play as well as Erica did. Erica had often told Caroline about her soccer team and how much she liked to play. This would be Caroline's first opportunity to actually see her friend in action.

How will I ever be able to make this decision?, she thought. ■

---

1. **Why is Caroline having such a difficult time trying to decide where she should be on Saturday afternoon?**
    A. Caroline is a person who always has trouble deciding anything.
    B. She really wants someone else just to tell her what to do.
    C. All three possibilities involve being with people who are important to her.
    D. Caroline would really rather be spending Saturday all by herself.

Could I use my own experience to help me answer this question?
- Have you ever had difficulty deciding ahead of time what to do when several things were possible?
- If you have, what made the decision so hard for you to make?

Look at all the choices and think about the one that best answers the question.

The question asks you to judge which choice can best be backed up by the information given in the paragraphs.

Is it answer choice A?
Is there enough about Caroline's personality in these paragraphs to let the reader know that this statement is true?

What about answer choice B?
Is Caroline's difficulty that she really wants someone else to make this decision for her? Is this what these paragraphs are saying?

Could it be answer choice C?
Are Caroline's feelings about being with her family, friends, classmates, and best friend causing her stress?

How about answer choice D?
Is there anything in the paragraphs to tell readers that Caroline would rather spend the afternoon by herself and not go to any of the three events?

Caroline is faced with choosing which very important persons or person she will spend Saturday afternoon with, so **C** is the correct answer.

DRAWING CONCLUSIONS

When you **draw a conclusion**, you make a statement about the meaning of something you have read about.

The word *draw* here does not mean sketching or making a picture; it means to "pull out." (If you draw on your imagination, you will surely write a creative story.) In order to draw a conclusion that makes sense, you must use strong evidence from the story or article.

To draw a conclusion, you should follow these steps:
• Start by identifying the main idea and supporting details.
• Think about what you already know about the topic.
• Put the information from the passage together with what you already know.

Once you have reached your conclusion, either go over in your mind what you have read or look back and review the passage.

LET'S TRY IT TOGETHER

DIRECTIONS   Read the story and together we will discuss the question.

Impressionists

Valerie, her friend Sophie, and their classmates were on the bus headed to the art museum. On the bus, their teacher Mrs. Graham told them, "Look at the flowers and trees you can see from the bus windows. This will prepare you for what you are going to see."

She had introduced them to the style of art called "Impressionism." The students were looking forward to seeing original paintings by some of the movement's important artists: Degas, Monet, Manet, and Renoir. Paintings in this style appear to be images of scenes that someone has just caught a glimpse of. They are bright, vibrant, and painted in bold colors.

After the class had gone inside the museum, Valerie noticed a sign announcing the Impressionist exhibit. A curator met the group there, welcomed them, and spoke for a few minutes about the exhibit. She told them to be very careful not to touch or get too close to any of the paintings. They could see a security guard standing nearby and keeping an eye on the visitors. Then Mrs. Graham said to them, "Because the museum isn't crowded today, we will have enough room to stand at different distances from each painting. An Impressionist painting will not look the same if you view it from about two feet away and then look at it again from five feet away. I will be around if anyone has questions."

As the group walked through the exhibit, Valerie suddenly stopped in front of a painting and gazed at the two girls portrayed in it. She motioned to Sophie for her to join her. The painting by Pierre-Auguste Renoir was titled "Girls Putting Flowers in Their Hats."

"Oh, how beautiful," whispered Sophie. Valerie nodded in agreement.

The girl on the right is wearing a hat. She is standing and bending over slightly as she adds brightly colored flowers to the other girl's yellow straw hat. The girl on the left in the painting is seated and also wearing a big hat. Her expression is pensive; she holds a flower in one hand, perhaps to hand to the other girl when she finishes putting in the one she has.

Valerie and Sophie stood there for what seemed a very long time, looking first at one girl and then at the other. After a while, Mrs. Graham announced that, before they left the museum, they would spend a little time visiting the gift shop.

In the gift shop Valerie was delighted to find a box of notecards with "Girls Putting Flowers in Their Hats" on them. *She would love these*, Valerie thought. She picked it up, carefully counted out her money, and paid for it at the counter. Standing behind her in line was Sophie, who had found a poster of a Monet print that she had liked. ∎

---

1. **For whom had Valerie most likely bought the notecards?**
   A. the curator
   B. Sophie
   C. Mrs. Graham
   D. her mom

To answer this question, you should follow some steps.

First, you should look for information within the text.

- A class goes on a field trip to an art exhibit at a local museum.
- The exhibit is made up of Impressionist paintings.
- Valerie and Sophie spend a long time admiring one painting.
- In the gift shop afterwards, Valerie finds notecards of that painting.

Then, think about your own experiences.

- Have you ever been to an art museum?
- Are there any art works or prints hanging up in your house?
- Do you like to look at paintings that you've never seen before?
- Have you ever seen something in a shop that either you wanted for yourself or thought of buying for someone else?

Finally, take a look at the choices mentioned in the answer options.

A. the curator

Could this be the answer? Is there anything in the story to indicate that Valerie might buy a gift for the museum curator? Think about the facts that you do know. This is probably not the best answer.

B. Sophie

Sophie did think the painting was beautiful. This may very well be the answer. However, remember to look at all the choices before you choose the one you think is right.

C. Mrs. Graham

While a teacher might use notecards and students sometimes give gifts to their teachers, is there anything in the story to show that this might be something that Mrs. Graham would appreciate? This is probably not the correct answer.

D. her mom

Is there anything in the paragraph to tell us that Valerie's mom would appreciate a gift like this? Nothing in the passage is directly connected to Valerie's mom.

Putting together all the information from the passage with your own experience, you should draw the conclusion that Valerie probably bought the notecards as a gift for Sophie, who seemed to be similarly in awe of its beauty. Answer choice **B** is correct.

YOU TRY IT

DIRECTIONS **INTRODUCTION** Read this story/passage and answer the questions that follow. The following editorial appeared in a local newspaper after the most recent Paralympics Games. The author of the article has a strong opinion about how the Paralympics should be treated by the media.

Point of View: The Paralympics

Sunday, January 8   **THE GLASSBORO GAZETTE**   F5

EDITORIAL
THE PARALYMPICS NEED RESPECT

Its time to give the Paralympics Games the respect they deserve. These games are the second largest sporting event in the world. Only the Olympics are larger. Yet, few people even know that they are held every two years. Almost no media coverage is given to the Paralympics Games.

Everyone knows about the Olympics. The media coverage starts years before the events are held. Even the choice of the host city for each Olympics is front-page news. Yet, there is no mention of the Paralympics in these news releases. No one is told that the Paralympics are held in the same host city two weeks later.

The Paralympics are just like the Olympics. World-class athletes train for years to be in both games. Then, the athletes compete to decide who will represent their country. In the actual races of both Olympics, the winners receive gold, silver, and bronze medals. The major difference between the two is that all the athletes in the Paralympics are disabled in some way.

4 The lack of respect shown toward the Paralympics is exhibited in many different ways. The host cities often do things to undercut the Paralympics. In Atlanta, for instance, the sponsors took down the booths in the Olympic Park right after the 1996 Olympics were over. By the time the Paralympics were held, consequently, the booths were gone. In another city, the Olympics took down their banners when they were done; all they left behind for the Paralympics was a blue line on the street.

In Sydney in 2000, almost the same thing happened. The Olympic rings were taken down right before the Paralympics started. In addition, on opening day of the Paralympics, that city held a large rally to thank the 43,000 Olympic volunteers. When told about the scheduling conflict, city officials refused to change the date of the event.

Even the raising of money is stacked against the Paralympics. The Paralympics cannot ask for funds from any competitor of an Olympic sponsor. Paralympics participants are therefore prevented from getting money from many private sponsors.

This lack of consideration and respect must come to an end. The Paralympics are equal to the Olympics. It is time that people gave them the equal esteem they deserve. We need the Olympics – both the Olympics and Paralympics – to work together. Officials should create a joint planning group. This group could then plan the two Olympic events together. It would ensure that both Olympics shared everything. While each Olympics would still keep its own rules committee, in most other things, they would cooperate with each other. The athletes from both Olympics would benefit from this joint effort.

Write to your local newspaper and express your opinion! Tell them that you want the two Olympics to work together in the future.

Sincerely, Thomas Krepowski

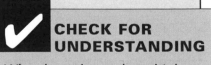

CHECK FOR UNDERSTANDING

Why does the author think that few people know about the Paralympics?

1. **Why did the author most likely write this passage?**
   A. to encourage people to show the Paralympics more respect
   B. to inform people about where the Paralympics will be held
   C. to help athletes of the Paralympics raise more money
   D. to support the idea of moving the date of the Paralympics

HINT: *This question asks you to identify the author's purpose. Think about what you have read. Why do you think the author decided to write this passage?*

2. **How are the Paralympics and the Olympics "alike"?**
   A. There is one committee for both competitions.
   B. The two events have many different sponsors.
   C. Both get the same amount of media coverage.
   D. Athletes train for years for both competitions.

HINT: *This question asks you to make a judgment based on the passage. Where did the author compare the two events? If you are unsure of the answer, skim the first column of the article.*

3. **The purpose of the fourth paragraph is to**
   A. show how two athletic competitions are similar.
   B. explain how host cities hurt the Paralympics.
   C. tell readers why the Olympics were started.
   D. show readers how athletes train for the Paralympics.

HINT: *This question asks you to identify why the author wrote a particular paragraph. Reread paragraph 4. What do you think the author was trying to say?*

4. **In paragraph 6, the word "funds" means**
   A. space.
   B. people.
   C. money.
   D. supplies.

HINT: *This question asks you to identify the meaning of the word "funds." Reread paragraph 6. Are there any clues to the word's meaning in the paragraph?*

5. How does the author think the problem can be solved?

    A. by allowing athletes from the Paralympics into the Olympic games

    B. by making a joint committee for the Olympics and Paralympics

    C. by holding the Olympics and Paralympics at the exact same time

    D. by giving the Paralympics more space than the Olympics

HINT: This question asks you to think about the information from the passage. If you are unsure of the answer, reread the end of the passage.

6. Which of the following does the author do last?

    A. The author asks people to help sponsor the Paralympics.

    B. The author tells people how host cities ignore the Paralympics.

    C. The author asks people to write to their local newspapers.

    D. The author tells people why the Paralympics are special to him.

HINT: This question asks you to recall the order in which the author organized the passage. If you are unsure of the answer, reread the end of the passage. You should look for the author's suggestions of a plan of action.

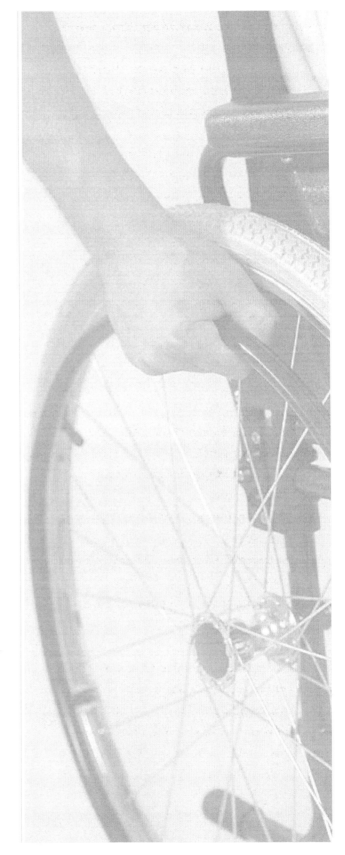

7. **This article was written with a specific purpose and opinion in mind.**
   • **What is the author's main opinion in this article? Explain.**
   • **In what ways does the author best support his views? Explain.**
   Use specific information from the article and any additional insight to support your response.

_____

_____

_____

_____

_____

_____

_____

_____

_____

_____

_____

_____

_____

_____

_____

_____

_____

_____

Explore CCSS/PARCC Grade 6 Reading

8. To improve things for the Paralympics, the author cites several areas where actions and rules have to change.
   • Name one area where change is needed so that the Paralympics will be more fairly presented to the public.
   • Which practical steps do you think should be taken to achieve the desired outcome? Explain.

   Use specific information from the article and any additional insight to support your response.

YOU TRY IT

DIRECTIONS INTRODUCTION	Read this story/passage and answer the questions that follow. Joshua L. Chamberlain, christened "Lawrence Joshua," was born on a farm in Brewer, Maine, in 1828. He was a professor, a soldier, a governor, a college president, and a port surveyor. In all these roles – as a leader and a man of principle and courage – he excelled.

Joshua Lawrence Chamberlain
A Man of Honor

By the age of 26, Joshua Chamberlain had graduated from Bowdoin College and Bangor Theological Seminary; he had thought of becoming a missionary. However, when he was offered a position teaching at Bowdoin College – a rare opportunity for such a young man at such a fine school – he accepted the position.

By 1862, Chamberlain was concerned about how certain issues of the day were dividing the Union. He had been following the news with interest, particularly since he believed in abolishing slavery. When the Civil War erupted, he informed the college that he wanted to enlist. They told him that he was more valuable as a teacher and would not approve of him leaving to join the military. Chamberlain then asked for a leave of absence to tour Europe and, when it was granted, signed up for the U.S. Army instead.

Chamberlain persuaded the governor of Maine to assign him to one of the state's regiments. He was offered the rank of colonel to head the 20th Maine regiment. While Chamberlain acknowledged that he was a master of foreign languages and other subjects, he also knew that he had not been trained as a soldier. Therefore, he accepted the rank of lieutenant colonel instead, second in command to Colonel Adelbert Ames. Ames was a West Point graduate and had already been named a hero after having been wounded in the war.

Chamberlain studied everything he could about warfare. He also carefully studied Colonel Ames as he trained and led the regiment. Before long, Ames was given a higher command and Chamberlain was in command of the 20th Maine.

While ill with malaria, Chamberlain faced a dilemma that threatened the lives of many. Men and even whole regiments could enlist to serve in the military for a given period of time. The 3rd Maine regiment had served its two years and was disbanded. However, about 100 men, who had joined late, still had time left to serve. They were to join the 20th Maine, and all but 60 did. Chamberlain's supporters told him to shoot anybody who did not join him; they would be considered deserters by the Union Army. By listening to their complaints, showing sympathy for their problems, and feeding them, however, Chamberlain was fortunately able to win over all but two of them.

5

Still suffering from illness, Chamberlain took command of his men in the Battle of Gettysburg. At a small hill, later named "Little Round Top," his was the last unit on the Union line. If this hill had been lost during the battle, the Confederate troops could have circled around behind the Union troops and attacked them from this weaker position. For the Union, the battle would have been lost.

The 20th Maine suffered many casualties as it repelled several assaults during the Battle of Gettysburg. Two bullets injured Chamberlain; one tore a gash in his foot, and the other hit his sword and badly bruised his thigh. Running out of ammunition, Chamberlain and his men fixed bayonets[1] to their rifles. They charged the Confederate forces and succeeded in driving back two regiments.

That night, another Union regiment refused to advance on a higher hill. (It became known as "Big Round Top.") Chamberlain was asked if his regiment would go instead; he agreed and asked for volunteers. Every one of the men still able to fight volunteered. So, with fewer than 200 soldiers, he advanced. They took the hill with little resistance. The next day, the Battle of Gettysburg ended in a Union victory. Much of the credit was given to the action of the 20th Maine on "Little Round Top."

8

In May 1864, Chamberlain was made brigade commander in the Army of the Potomac. During the Battle of Petersburg, which followed soon thereafter, Chamberlain was struck by a bullet that entered his right hip and traveled through his lower body to his left hip. His wound was so serious that he was left for dead. He even wrote a farewell letter to his wife Fanny. Several generals came to say their goodbyes. General Ulysses S. Grant learned of Chamberlain's serious condition and awarded him the rank of brigadier general.

[1]**bayonet** *a knife-, dagger-, or spike-shaped weapon attached to a riffle barrel and used in hand-to-hand combat.*

Chamberlain's brother Tom, who was with the 20th Maine, heard about his brother's injury. He brought two doctors to try to save him. They did what they could and he was then sent to the Naval Academy hospital in Annapolis, Maryland. A long recovery followed. However, pain and recurring infections were to plague him for the rest of his life. Nevertheless, despite great discomfort, he miraculously returned to the war the following year.

General Chamberlain and his horse were wounded again in the Battle of Quaker Road. Still he led his men in a charge. Two days later, he was asked to lead another charge against Confederate General Robert E. Lee. Chamberlain was to recapture the road his men had taken two days before. He mounted his wounded horse and led his men into battle. It ended with the capture of an entire Confederate regiment.

General Lee's surrender at Appomattox marked the end of the long Civil War. General Grant chose Chamberlain to accept the surrender of the Confederate Army Infantry. Even though he knew that many northerners would be upset, as the Confederate units laid down their arms and passed before the Union troops, Chamberlain ordered that a salute be given. He felt that the brave men deserved honor and he hoped to help begin the healing process for the nation.

General Chamberlain left the army in 1866, having been in 24 skirmishes and battles. He returned to his home in Brunswick, Maine. As a popular war hero, he was asked to run for governor. He did and won by a huge margin. He served for four one-year terms. Not a politician, he failed to side with his party on several issues. Unfortunately, as a result of these views, he made many enemies.

Chamberlain returned to Bowdoin College as president for the next 12 years. He believed in a well-rounded education. He introduced many new courses and set up a science department. He also wanted women to be admitted to the college, but he could never reach this goal. He also thought that the army would need more trained leaders in case of war, so he included military training as part of students' schoolwork. Later, when several classes refused to train, the men involved were expelled. Chamberlain managed to devise a compromise that would allow these same students to return to the college, and all but two did return.

In 1879, Maine faced a serious problem with their state election. Two groups each claimed victory for seats in the legislature. The governor would be chosen by whichever side held a majority of the seats. Anger grew and a civil war became a serious threat. The governor called upon Chamberlain for help. Rather than call in the local militia, Chamberlain met with both sides. He suggested that they send their arguments to Maine's Supreme Court to have them decide the winners.

For 12 days, Chamberlain, the mayor of Augusta, and the local police kept the peace. There were threats to Chamberlain's life. At one point, he went out to face a mob set to kill him. He told them he wanted to see the rightful government seated. He said, "I am here for that, and I shall do it. If anybody wants to kill me for it, here I am. Let him kill!"

A veteran in the mob shouted, "By God, old General, the first man that dares to lay a hand on you, I'll kill him on the spot." With that, the crowd disbanded. The court settled the matter and Maine was spared its civil war. Again, Chamberlain had made powerful enemies.

When a seat on the United States Senate became open, Chamberlain was the logical choice for the job. However, the people did not elect senators at that time; instead, they were chosen by the state legislature. Chamberlain's enemies finally saw an opportunity to get their revenge. They named someone else to the Senate.

Chamberlain ended his career as a port surveyor in Portland, Maine. He was all but forgotten except by those who had fought in the Civil War. It was 30 years after the Battle of Gettysburg before he was awarded the Congressional Medal of Honor. Our country's highest honor arrived in a package delivered by a postman.

Chamberlain died at the age of eighty-five, 50 years after he had been given up for dead. Joshua Lawrence Chamberlain was a man of great courage, high principles, and remarkable leadership skills. He is a man of honor well worth remembering. ∎

1. **Which of the following statements best describes the author's attitude toward Chamberlain?**
   A. The author admires Chamberlain.
   B. The author is jealous of Chamberlain.
   C. The author distrusts Chamberlain.
   D. The author is afraid of Chamberlain.

   HINT: *This question asks you to make a judgment based on the passage. Based on what you have read, what do you think is the author's opinion?*

2. **Why did Chamberlain refuse to command the 20th Maine regiment at first?**
   A. He wanted to achieve a higher rank.
   B. He couldn't leave his teaching position.
   C. He wanted to command a larger force.
   D. He didn't feel prepared to do it.

   HINT: *This question asks you to think about information from the passage. If you are unsure of the answer, reread the third paragraph.*

3. **Which of the following best describes Chamberlain in the fifth paragraph?**
   A. cruel
   B. cooperative
   C. brave
   D. welcoming

   HINT: *This question asks you to think about information from the passage. If you are unsure of the answer, reread the fifth paragraph.*

4. **What does the word "disbanded" mean in paragraph 5?**
   A. relocated
   B. make up
   C. punished
   D. break up

   HINT: *This question asks you to identify the meaning of the word "disbanded." Reread paragraph 5. Are there any clues to the words meaning in the sentence?*

5. Who helped to save Chamberlain's life?
   A. doctors sent by the Naval Academy hospital
   B. doctors assigned to his Pennsylvania First Brigade
   C. doctors his brother brought from the 20th Maine
   D. doctors sent by the governor of Maine

HINT: This question asks you to recall a detail. If you are unsure of the answer, reread the tenth paragraph.

6. Which of the following best describes Chamberlain in the eighth paragraph?
   A. upbeat
   B. cautious
   C. determined
   D. humorous

HINT: This question asks you to think about information from the passage. If you are unsure of the answer, reread the eighth paragraph.

7. Which event happened right after Chamberlain left the army?
   A. He became a port surveyor in Portland.
   B. He became governor of Maine.
   C. He helped Maine prevent a civil war.
   D. He became president of Bowdoin College.

HINT: This question asks you to recall a detail from the passage. If you are unsure of the answer, reread the middle of the passage.

8. What was the most likely reason that Chamberlain was not chosen to serve in the U.S. Senate?
   A. He was not someone who could be told how to vote.
   B. He was not well known in the state of Maine.
   C. He had not been trained as a lawyer.
   D. He was not familiar with the workings of government.

HINT: This question asks you to make a judgment based on information in the passage. If you are unsure of the answer, reread the end of the passage, looking for a mention about Chamberlain's run for the Senate.

9. Joshua Lawrence Chamberlain earned the respect of many people throughout his lifetime.
   • Identify one instance when people showed respect for Chamberlain.
   • How did this event demonstrate that people respected him? Explain.
   Use specific information from the article and any additional insight to support your response.

10. A person willing to stand up for what he or she believes in will often be wholeheartedly supported or strongly disputed.
    • Of the choices that Joshua Lawrence Chamberlain made during his life, which one would you either support or dispute? Explain.
    Use specific information from the article and any additional insight to support your response.

YOU TRY IT

What Is Braille?

Braille is the code used by blind and visually impaired people to read and write. People who are blind or whose eyesight is very poor use their fingers to read a series of raised dots on a piece of paper.

The Braille System of Writing

Every character in the Braille code is based on an arrangement of one to six raised dots in a rectangle called a Braille cell. Each dot has a numbered position in the cell. *Figure 1* shows a Braille cell on the left and the numbers given to each of the dots on the right.

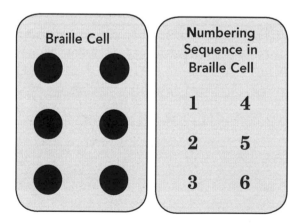

FIGURE 1: *Each of the dots is given a number. The upper left dot is known as number 1; the upper right is known as number 4. The letter "d" is written with the number one, four, and five dots raised.*

Each letter of the alphabet has its own rectangle of raised dots to represent that letter. Louis Braille perfected the use of the raised bumps on the page while he was a student at the French School for the Blind in Paris.

There are no different symbols for capital letters in Braille. Capital letters are indicated by placing a dot in the sixth spot of a Braille cell just before the letter that is capitalized. This tells the reader that the next letter is a capital letter.

If the entire word is capitalized, two cells with a dot in the sixth spot of a Braille cell will precede the word. *Figure 2* shows how the dots are arranged in the Braille cell for each letter of the alphabet.

About 25 lines of 40 Braille cells will fit on a piece of Braille paper that is either 11 inches wide by 11 inches long or 11 inches wide by 12 inches long. This allows about 1,000 Braille characters to be written per page, as opposed to about 3,500 typed words on letter-sized (8 1/2" x 11") paper. Braille paper is a heavier weight than regular paper in order to hold the Braille

5

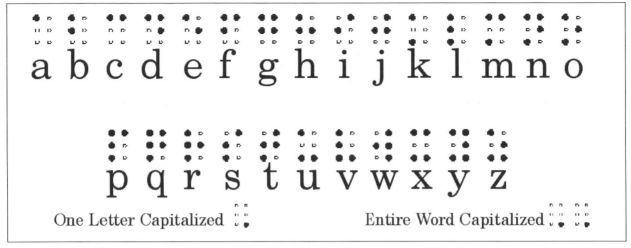

FIGURE 2: Grade 1 Braille

dots. Therefore, Braille books are thicker and heavier than regular printed books.

Over the years, countries have made modifications to the Braille code to reduce the size of the books and to increase the speed at which people read and write the language. However, all forms of the Braille code use some system of six raised dots in a rectangle to represent various letters. Nonetheless, different methods are used by different countries to represent more common words and/or letters.

Braille Systems Used in the U.S.

There are two basic systems of Braille used in the United States: Grade 1 Braille and Grade 2 Braille. The use of Grade 1 and Grade 2 for Braille has nothing to do with grades in school. These terms mean different types of Braille. Grade 1 Braille is a direct substitution of every print letter in a given book or article. However, few

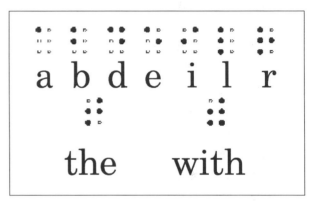

FIGURE 3: Example of Grade 2 Braille

books or written materials are translated into this form of Braille because it results in extremely thick books.

Grade 2 Braille *(Figure 3)* is the Braille code more commonly used in the United States. It is a shorter form of Braille, which makes reading and writing the language much faster. Many of the individual letters are still represented by specific cells. However, some of the cells are also used individually or in combination with others to form 189 letter contractions and 76 whole words.

For example, in Braille 2, the letter "y" represents the word "you." The letter "l" is used to represent the word "like." The cells representing contractions and whole words must be memorized. However, once a student has learned them, he or she can read Braille much faster. Books written in Grade 2 Braille are not as bulky as those written in Grade 1 Braille.

Writing of Braille

There are two methods used for writing Braille. One is with a Braille writing machine and the other is with a slate and stylus. *Figure 4* shows a Braille writer. It has six keys, one for each dot that can be pushed either separately or all together. A spacebar key is located midway between the six dot keys. Pushing various combinations of keys makes the different dot combinations for the Braille letters.

The second method is writing Braille with a slate and stylus. The slate or template has evenly spaced depressions for dots of Braille cells in a line across the page. Braille paper is placed in the slate. Pushing the pointed end of the stylus into the paper over the properly numbered depressions makes the dots. The paper bulges on the other side, showing the dots. The person taking notes writes from right to left. Then the paper is turned over in order to be read. A person would read the paper from left to right, just as a sighted person would ordinarily read. The speed of writing Braille this way is about the same as the speed of writing print with a pencil. ■

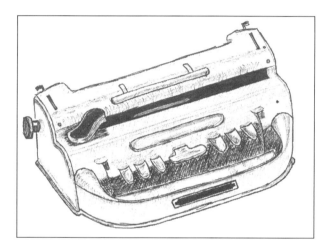

FIGURE 4: Braille Writer

1. **What about a Braille cell tells the person which letter is being spelled?**
   A. the size of the dots
   B. the placement of the dots
   C. the shape of the Braille cell
   D. the number of Braille cells

   HINT: *This question asks you to recall a detail from the passage. If you are unsure of the answer, reread the "Braille System of Writing" section.*

2. **In paragraph 5, the word "precede" means**
   A. look after.
   B. hold up.
   C. move around.
   D. come before.

   HINT: *This question asks you to identify the meaning of the word "precede." Reread paragraph 5. Are there any clues to the word's meaning in the paragraph?*

3. **How are capital letters recognized in Braille writing?**
   A. as a separate cell for each letter
   B. in the second cell before the letter
   C. in the cell before the letter
   D. in two cells after the letter

   HINT: *This question asks you to recall a detail from the passage. If you are unsure of the answer, reread the fourth paragraph.*

4. **How are Braille books and print books alike?**
   A. Both are read left to right.
   B. Both use regular-sized paper.
   C. Both are usually very thick.
   D. Both contain very few words.

   HINT: *This question asks you to draw a conclusion based on the passage. Think about what the author told you about Braille books. What about them is similar to print books?*

5. **Why are many books today written using Braille Grade 2?**
    A. Few people can read Braille Grade 1 today.
    B. Fewer words are misspelled by using Braille Grade 2.
    C. Using Braille Grade 2 makes reading much faster.
    D. Braille Grade 1 is only written in France.

HINT: This question asks you to think about information from the passage. What did the passage say about Braille Grade 2 that might explain why many books are written using this format today?

6. **What could make Braille Grade 2 a problem for some people?**
    A. It is totally different from Braille Grade 1.
    B. They have to memorize some Braille shortcuts.
    C. They have to learn how to use a Braille writer.
    D. It uses many more dots than Braille Grade 1.

HINT: This question asks you to make a judgment based on what you have read in the passage. If you are unsure of the answer, think back to what the passage told you about Braille Grade 2.

7. **What is one difference between using the Braille writer and using a slate and stylus?**
    A. A Braille writer uses six dots for a cell.
    B. A Braille writer uses Braille Grade 1.
    C. A Braille writer is much more accurate.
    D. A Braille writer types letters faster.

HINT: This question asks you to make a judgment about the passage. Based on what you have read, what difference can you recognize between the tools used for writing Braille?

8. **Why did the author most likely write this passage?**
    A. to explain how people use Braille to read and write
    B. to encourage the reader to read and write using Braille
    C. to describe how the two grades of Braille are different
    D. to convince people to learn to use Braille Grade 2

HINT: This question asks you to think about why the author wrote the passage. Think about what you have read. What do you think the author was trying to say?

9. Braille is a language just like any other. It is simply crafted differently.
   - If you were writing a message using a Braille writer, how would the technique differ from the way you would ordinarily write something?
   - Why does Braille have to be written that way? Explain.

   Use specific information from the article and any additional insight to support your response.

10. Along with the people who are blind or visually impaired, some sighted people learn to read and write Braille.

   • After reading this passage, would you be interested in learning more about Braille? Explain.

   • In what kinds of jobs would it be important for someone to know how to read and write Braille? Explain.

   Use specific information from the article and any additional insight to support your response.

YOU TRY IT

| **DIRECTIONS** | Read this story/passage and answer the questions that follow. |
| **INTRODUCTION** | This passage tells about a sea monster that has been said to exist for centuries. Could it be real? |

The Kraken Sea Monster

Sailors have feared the legendary Kraken for centuries. According to stories, this sea monster with many arms could reach as high as the top of a sailing ship's main mast. Sailors believed that the Kraken would wrap its arms around a ship and either pull it down or capsize it.

Figure 1

The first time this type of sea monster appeared in a story was in Homer's *Odyssey*. A monster with many arms guarded Scylla's home as the main character, Odysseus, sailed past. The monster was also mentioned in two very early history books about Scandinavia. The Vikings called this monster the Kraken.

The Vikings said that the Kraken was a horned sea monster. They described it as being so large that sailors sometimes mistook it for an island. Other sailors, when they ventured closer, saw what appeared to be many heads and large, waving arms like tentacles. Sometimes, the Kraken was said to discharge an inky liquid into the surrounding waters. Sailors thought that this liquid poisoned the water.

In later years, however, people began to dismiss the Kraken legend. The few reports about large sea animals told of long snake-like animals swimming alone in the water. In 1915, a gigantic sea animal was seen on the surface for about 15 seconds. There was no mention of a monster with many arms. Many people started to call the story of the Kraken sea monster "a tall tale told by scared sailors."

4

One day, two boys saw what appeared to be a big blob of something on a beach in Florida. The body was badly mutilated and only a portion of the creature remained. Examination led scientists to believe that the full creature might have had a body over 100 feet across. The arms were 18 inches around and may have been 75 to 100 feet long. This had been a colossal sea animal!

At first, people thought that the boys had found the carcass of a whale. Later, scientists decided it was a member of the cephalopod family. Many thought it was a huge octopus. However, since no other octopi this size had ever been found, no one was really sure what the boys had found on the beach that November day.

7 In the 1930s, some yachts reported being attacked by large sea animals with many arms. However, the animals always broke off the encounters when they slid into the ship's propellers. Yet, the fact that they had attacked a ship at all made people wonder once again about the Kraken legend.

Most authorities thought that the animals attacking the yachts were giant squid. While similar to an octopus, the squid is more aggressive. Squid also spend their time in the middle depths of the ocean. The octopus is a bottom dweller. Octopi use their arms to move from rock to rock along the bottom of the ocean.

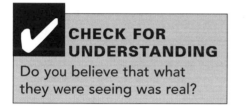

✔ CHECK FOR UNDERSTANDING
Do you believe that what they were seeing was real?

In April 2003, the legend of the Kraken took another turn. Fishermen off the coast of Antarctica caught a huge squid that had eyes the size of dinner plates. It also had scores of razor-sharp hooks on its tentacles. These fishermen had caught a half-grown female colossal squid.

Scientists believed that these sea animals had existed for some time; however, they had never seen one. Previously, pieces of what was thought to have been such a creature were found inside the stomachs of sperm whales. These discoveries did lead scientists to theorize that there was a type of squid that was larger and more dangerous than the giant squid, and they called this one colossal squid. The finding of a half-grown female by the fishermen proved the scientists to be correct. There was, in fact, a squid larger than the giant squid. A colossal squid weighs over a ton and is more than 20 yards long. Its arms can reach over 75 feet. (*Figure 1* shows the size of the colossal squid.)

Marine biologists say that the colossal squid is a very dangerous animal. It is very aggressive and moves quickly. Its eight arms and two tentacles have up to 25 teeth-like claws in addition to large suckers on the tentacles. The razor-sharp claws can rotate up to 360 degrees. These hooks are used both to hold fish and to fight off sperm whales. The colossal squid finds its food by glowing in the deep water of the ocean. The glow lights up its prey, and the squid is then able to see it with its large eyes. These eyes are the biggest of any known animal.

Today, people think that sailors base the Kraken legend upon sightings of colossal squids. These squids have many arms and squirt ink into the ocean. Though they are not a mile across (as in the legends), colossal squids are certainly large enough to wrestle with a sperm whale. ∎

1. By whom was the Kraken sea monster first mentioned?

A. Homer

B. the Vikings

C. two boys

D. fishermen

HINT: *This question asks you to recall a detail from the passage. If you are unsure of the answer, reread the second paragraph.*

2. According to stories, how big was the Kraken?

A. as big as a building

B. as big as a ship

C. as big as a horse

D. as big as a snake

HINT: *This question asks you to recall a detail from the passage. If you are unsure of the answer, reread paragraph 1.*

3. The purpose of the fourth paragraph is to

A. explain how the mystery of the Kraken was solved.

B. describe what people believed the Kraken looked like.

C. tell why many believed that the Kraken was a myth.

D. show readers why many sailors feared the Kraken.

HINT: *This question asks you to identify why the author wrote a particular paragraph. Reread paragraph 4. What do you think the author was trying to say?*

4. What did people believe the boys on the beach had found?

A. a plant

B. a fish

C. a squid

D. a whale

HINT: *This question asks you to identify why the author wrote a particular paragraph. Reread paragraph 4. What do you think the author was trying to say?*

5. What caused people to become interested in the Kraken legend again?

A. things found in a sperm whale's stomach

B. the discovery two boys made at a beach

C. a giant sea creature spotted on the surface

D. reports of a creature that attacked yachts

HINT: *This question asks you to make a judgment based on the passage. Think about when the author mentioned a renewed interest in the legend.*

6. What does the word "encounters" mean in paragraph 7?

A. sails

B. rocks

C. meetings

D. mysteries

HINT: *This question asks you to identify the meaning of the word "encounters." Reread the paragraph 7. Are there any clues to the word's meaning in the paragraph?*

7. How are the giant squid and colossal squid different?

A. The colossal squid is a bottom-dweller.

B. The colossal squid is a much larger squid.

C. The colossal squid is much less aggressive.

D. The colossal squid has never been seen.

HINT: *This question asks you to make a judgment about what you have read in the passage. If you are unsure of the answer, skim the passage looking for a mention of the colossal squid.*

8. Which part of the colossal squid is most dangerous?

A. its glow

B. its claws

C. its eyes

D. its ink

HINT: *This question asks you to think about information from the passage. If you are unsure of the answer, reread the end of the passage.*

9. It happens every once in a while that a creature largely believed to be purely legendary happens to be a real beast after all.
   • How might it have been possible for the colossal squid to remain undiscovered for so long? Explain.
   Use specific information from the article and any additional insight to support your response.

10. One meaning of the word "colossal" is "so great in size or force or extent as to elicit awe."
    • Do you think the right name was chosen for the colossal squid? Explain.
    • Which other living being or inanimate object would you describe as "colossal"? Explain.
    Use specific information from the article and any additional insight to support your response.

_____

_____

_____

_____

_____

_____

_____

_____

_____

_____

_____

_____

_____

YOU TRY IT

DIRECTIONS **INTRODUCTION**	Read this story/passage and answer the questions that follow. This is the story of the whaling ship *Essex*. It was the only ship ever known to have been sunk by a whale.

The *Essex*

In the summer of 1819, the whaling ship *Essex* left Nantucket, Massachusetts. It was heading out on a two-and-a-half-year voyage to the South Pacific in search of the aggressive sperm whale.

Before the *Essex* set sail, several events occurred that made people think that this would be an unlucky trip. First, only days before the voyage, a blazing comet had streaked across the sky. Swarms of grasshoppers also appeared and ate many of the crops in the fields. There were also repeated sightings of a so-called sea monster in the water off Nantucket. However, 28-year-old Captain George Pollard, Jr. was not superstitious and sailed on schedule.

After having been at sea for only two days, the *Essex* was knocked over by a sudden squall. The ship lay completely on its side for several minutes before righting itself. The crew was very upset and wanted to turn back. Since no damage had been done to the ship, however, the captain ordered that they continue on to the South Pacific.

Once there, the *Essex*'s luck changed. The crew caught several whales and filled half the ship's barrels with sperm oil. Then disaster struck.

4

On November 20, 1820, lookouts spotted a pod of whales. Three boats were lowered and set off toward the whales. The tail of a whale damaged one boat soon after it reached the pod and it returned to the *Essex* for repairs. The other two boats continued to chase the whales.

The damaged boat was hauled aboard the ship and repairs were started. Suddenly, a sailor noticed a very large bull sperm whale starting to swim toward the *Essex*. Everyone expected him to swerve away before reaching the ship. However, the creature continued toward it, gaining speed as he approached. The *Essex* attempted to avoid the whale; nevertheless, it rammed the ship just past its bow. The force of the whale hitting the *Essex* stopped its forward motion. The whale swam away and seemed to go into convulsions. Then he stopped shaking, turned toward the *Essex*, and started swimming toward it again. The whale struck the *Essex* again, making a large hole below the water line. The whale backed away and then sank from sight.

The *Essex* began to take on water and slowly list to port (the left-hand side of the ship). As the other two boats returned to the ship, the men were appalled to find the *Essex* so badly damaged. Just as they reached the ship, it rolled over onto its side.

The 20-member crew immediately set about cutting away the masts of the ship. The *Essex* was then able to right itself. They were able to keep it afloat for several more days. The men knew that they would have to abandon ship. They packed the three smaller boats with only the supplies they thought they would need to keep them alive and started their epic journey back to the coast of South America. The crew left the *Essex* on November 22nd.

On December 20th, the three whaleboats reached small Henderson Island. The men went ashore and ate whatever they could find. Soon it became apparent that there was not enough food on the island to feed everyone. The crew made preparations to continue their journey. Three men, however, decided to remain on the island because they thought it was safer. On December 26th, the 17 remaining crewmen set sail once again in the three whaleboats. They were heading toward Easter Island.

✔ CHECK FOR UNDERSTANDING

Why do you think the author talks about each event in such great detail?

The boats soon ran into a series of storms. While the rain provided much-needed drinking water, the wind caused them to miss Easter Island. When the men realized their misfortune, they considered turning back, but since the winds would be against them if they went back to Easter Island, they continued on toward the coast of South America. What they didn't realize was that the coast of South America was 2,500 miles away. In another set of storms, the three boats got separated from each other. Each boat then continued on its own towards the continent.

In the next several weeks, the men in the boats became weaker and suffered from various illnesses. Their food, even on one-quarter rations, was perilously low. The men ate barnacle-like growths off the hulls of their longboats to stay alive. Even this was not enough and the men grew weaker. They were so exhausted that just lying in the boats was the limit of what they could do. Because of the exposure to the sun, lack of water, and extremely limited rations, no one had any energy to do anything. The first death occurred on January 10, 1821, and the body was buried at sea. Other deaths soon followed.

11

One boat, containing the captain and several other crew members, was rescued by the Nantucket whale ship *Dauphin* 95 days after the *Essex* sank. The British merchantman brig *Indian* rescued a second boat. The third boat was never found. The three men who had been left on Henderson Island were rescued several weeks later. They were desperately malnourished and ill. In all, eight men were rescued.

When the crew returned to Nantucket, they were hailed as heroes. Following the tragedy, all but one of the sailors and officers returned to sea. Most became successful captains of sailing or whaling ships.

The story of the *Essex* became a legend and is known to almost everyone who sails the oceans. Some of the crew even wrote stories of the horrifying events. It also served as the inspiration for Herman Melville's novel *Moby Dick*. Today, staff members of the Nantucket Historical Association retell the story of this ill-fated ship to visitors almost daily. ■

1. **Which of the following best describes the captain of the _Essex_?**
   A. cautious
   B. fearful
   C. determined
   D. anxious

   HINT: _This question asks you characterize a person mentioned in the passage. Think about what the author said about the captain of the Essex. Which of the answer options is the best?_

2. **What happened first to the ship and the crew once the ship left Nantucket?**
   A. The crew saw a sea monster nearby.
   B. The crew saw a comet in the sky.
   C. The ship was hit twice by a bull whale.
   D. The ship was hit by a sudden squall.

   HINT: _This question asks you to recall a detail from the passage. If you are unsure of the answer, reread paragraph 3._

3. **How did the boat sink?**
   A. A whale landed on the boat as it was jumping over it.
   B. A blazing comet from the sky crashed into the boat.
   C. A whale hit the boat and made a hole below the water line.
   D. The men cut the masts off the boat and it blew off course.

   HINT: _This question asks you to identify a detail. Reread paragraph 6. What does the author say?_

4. **What does the word "swerve" mean in paragraph 6?**
   A. die
   B. turn
   C. eat
   D. sink

   HINT: _This question asks you to identify the meaning of the word "swerve." Reread paragraph 6. Are there any clues to the word's meaning in the paragraph?_

5. Why was the crew unable to reach Easter Island?

   A. A whale had attacked and sunk the *Essex*.

   B. The crew ran out of food on the trip.

   C. The crew cut down ship's masts.

   D. A storm blew the boats off course.

HINT: This question asks you to recall a detail from the passage. If you are unsure of the answer, reread paragraph 10.

6. In paragraph 11, what does the author mean when he says, the food "even on one-quarter rations" was low?

   A. Everyone on board had enough food to eat.

   B. A quarter of the men were unable to eat.

   C. The men had to pay a quarter to eat food.

   D. Each man ate only one-fourth of the food he would normally eat.

HINT: This question asks you to predict what the author meant by a particular phrase. If you are unsure of the answer, reread paragraph 11. Are they any clues to the phrase's meaning in the paragraph?

7. How many men were eventually rescued?

   A. three

   B. five

   C. eight

   D. twenty

HINT: This question asks you to recall a detail from the passage. If you are unsure of the answer, reread the end of the paragraph.

8. The purpose of the fourth paragraph is to

   A. make the reader worry about when disaster will strike.

   B. show that the men had success hunting whales at first.

   C. encourage the reader to wonder what happened to the whale oil.

   D. tell about the problems the men had in the Pacific Ocean.

HINT: This question asks you to think about why the author wrote a certain paragraph. Reread paragraph 4. What do you think the author was trying to say?

9. The author explains how a few men decided to stay behind on Henderson Island rather than brave the long journey to South America.
   • Why do you think some of the men thought it was safer to stay on the island? Explain.
   • Do you think that it really was, in fact, safer? Explain.
   Use specific information from the article and any additional insight to support your response.

10. Today, most of the news about whales has shifted to what can be done to protect and save the remaining species from extinction.
    • As whale hunters, how do you think the sailors felt about protecting whales? Explain.
    • Do you think measures should be taken to protect whales? Explain.
    Use specific information from the article and any additional insight to support your response.

YOU TRY IT

DIRECTIONS INTRODUCTION	Read this story/passage and answer the questions that follow. John's family has moved into an area prone to being struck by hurricanes. In the town library, he found this pamphlet about how a family should prepare for a hurricane.

Preparing for a Hurricane

Types of Hurricanes

A hurricane is a tropical storm with winds that blow at 74 miles per hour or higher. Hurricanes begin as tropical storms and become more powerful as they move across the ocean. *Figure 1* shows the wind speed and level of potential damage for the five categories of hurricanes:

Category	Wind Speed (mph)	Damage
1	74–95	Minor
2	96–110	Moderate
3	111–130	Major
4	131–155	Severe
5	Above 155	Catastrophic

Figure 1

2 As a hurricane approaches, information about its track will be broadcast over the local radio and TV stations. Several phrases will be used to tell how close a hurricane is to a certain area. It is important to know what these phrases mean. They provide important information about making good decisions before and during oncoming storms. *Figure 2* lists these phrases:

Hurricane Watch:	A hurricane is coming toward the area and might arrive within 36 hours.
Hurricane Warning:	A hurricane is expected to strike the area within 24 hours. Preparations for surviving the storm should be completed as soon as this warning is heard.
Evacuation Order:	This tells you to leave the area quickly as possible. Once this order is given, it must be obeyed. It is the most important instruction given prior to the storm.

Figure 2

Preparing a Hurricane Disaster Plan

Each family should prepare a disaster plan to follow if a hurricane strikes their area. Knowledge of hurricanes is not enough by itself. It is important to develop both a hurricane disaster plan and a survival kit. Remember to prepare for the worst. That way, regardless of the severity of the hurricane, you will ensure your safety.

The first thing to do when developing a disaster plan is to decide whether or not your house can withstand a hurricane's strong winds. Consider these questions:

Was your house originally built to be strong enough to withstand these winds?

In recent years, hurricane-building standards have been developed for affected regions of the country. These standards will help you determine whether or not your house can withstand the winds from the various categories of hurricane. Determine if your house is up to code before making a decision. If you live in a mobile or manufactured home, plan to go to a safer place when a hurricane threatens. These types of houses are not good places to be during a hurricane.

Is your house located on ground high enough to not flood from the rains that accompany a hurricane?

If your house is prone to flooding or in an area that has been flooded in previous hurricanes, plan to leave when the hurricane is approaching.

If you decide it will be necessary to leave your home, decide where you will go during a hurricane. Several options are available to you. You could stay with nearby friends or relatives. Remember to ask your friends or relatives first if you can stay with them if that is what you plan to do! You could also leave the area completely. You might even decide to go to a public shelter in your area.

The next thing to do is to prepare an evacuation route. Determine several routes you can use to reach the locations you have chosen. It is very possible that, when the emergency occurs, one of your routes will be blocked by flooding or falling debris.

6

The last step is to actually get out and drive the various routes you have identified. See if they go through areas that flood in a heavy rain. Look for heavily wooded areas where trees could block the road. Determine which route would be best to take during a hurricane.

Making a Disaster Survival Kit

8 The other thing that must be done is to make a survival kit. Prepare your kit as if you will be staying in your house. If you leave, you will only take parts of it with you. However, if you are forced to remain in your house, you will have sufficient supplies for you and your family until the municipal services are restored.

The kit should include sufficient provisions so you can live without electricity, city water, city sewer, and other services for at least one week following a hurricane. Use water-resistant containers to store your supplies. Remember to check the kit periodically to ensure that things are working and to see what needs to be restocked.

Figure 3 is a list of items often included in survival kits. It is only a sample listing; people should add any other items that they feel may be important in an emergency.

Summary

When a hurricane does strike your area, remember to implement the plan you have developed. Remain calm until the emergency has ended. ■

Survival Kit List

- Water: *one gallon per person daily*
- Medicines: *prescriptions and over-the-counter medicines*
- First aid kit and booklet
- Food: *non-perishable foods that family members need to live for at least one week*
- Blankets and several changes of clothes
- Flashlights: *one for each family member*
- Portable radio
- Batteries: *for flashlights and radio*
- Water purification kit
- Non-electric can opener
- Toilet paper, paper towels, pre-moistened towelettes
- Eating utensils
- Mosquito repellent and citronella candle
- Eyeglasses
- Portable lantern and batteries or fuel
- Games or activities for children

Figure 3

1. **In the eighth paragraph, what does the reader learn about disaster kits?**
   A. You will only take part of your kit if you leave your home.
   B. You should have non-perishable foods in your disaster kit.
   C. The kit should never leave your home in an emergency.
   D. The kit should be kept inside the trunk of your automobile.

   HINT: This question asks you think about information from the passage. If you are unsure of the answer, reread the eighth paragraph. What did you learn?

2. **Why should you remain calm in an emergency?**
   A. You should already have a disaster kit.
   B. You can follow other cars to evacuate.
   C. It will make the hurricane less dangerous.
   D. It will help you make better decisions.

   HINT This question asks you to clarify information from the passage. Think about what the passage said while you read the answer options. Which of your choices best describes why you should remain calm in an emergency?

3. **Why is it important to know about the construction of your house?**
   A. It will tell you whether or not your house is really a mobile home.
   B. It will help determine whether or not to stay there.
   C. It will help you determine how to avoid bad damage.
   D. It will show you how to get help to rebuild the house.

   HINT: This question asks you to draw a conclusion based on the passage. If you are unsure of the answer, reread the bullet points of the "Preparing a Hurricane Disaster Plan" section of the passage.

4. **How many categories of hurricanes exist?**
   A. 3
   B. 5
   C. 74
   D. 155

   HINT: This question asks you to recall a detail from the passage. If you are unsure of the answer, refer back to Figure 1.

5. The purpose of the second paragraph is to

A. introduce Figure 2.

B. list television stations.

C. describe hurricane strength.

D. explain when to leave.

HINT: This question asks you to think about why the author wrote a certain paragraph. Reread paragraph 2. What do you think the author was trying to say?

6. What does the word "debris" mean in paragraph 6?

A. tree branches

B. water droplets

C. remains of something destroyed

D. friends, family, or homes

HINT: This question asks you to identify the meaning of the word "debris." Reread the paragraph 6. Are there any clues to the word's meaning in the paragraph?

7. Why should you drive the various escape routes you have planned ahead of time?

A. to know the roads so that you will not become lost

B. to keep from sightseeing during an emergency

C. to determine how many lanes are on each road

D. to determine if these areas could have problems

HINT: This question asks you to draw a conclusion based on the passage. If you are unsure of the answer, reread the last paragraph of the "Preparing a Hurricane Disaster Plan" section of the passage.

8. Why is a disaster plan important?

A. It will help you keep a disaster survival kit at home.

B. It will help you know which roads are safe for travel.

C. It will help you know what to do in a hurricane.

D. It will help you keep your house safe in a storm.

HINT: This question asks you to recall a detail from the passage. If you are unsure of the answer, reread the "Preparing a Hurricane Disaster Plan" section of the passage.

9. In the section "Making a Disaster Survival Kit," the author lists games and activities for children as part of *Figure 3*.

   • Why should you include games and activities for children in your family's disaster kit? Explain.

   Use specific information from the article and any additional insight to support your response.

---

10. The passage says that you might plan to stay with nearby friends or family during a hurricane.
    • Why do you think that the author recommends doing this? Explain.
    • Do you think this is a good idea? Explain.
    Use specific information from the article and any additional insight to support your response.

Made in the USA
San Bernardino, CA
23 June 2014